REVISED EDITION

Writing Scripts Hollywood Will Love

Katherine Atwell Herbert

ALLWORTH PRESS
NEW YORK

05 04 03 02 01 00   5 4 3 2 1

Published by Allworth Press
An imprint of Allworth Communications
10 East 23rd Street, New York, NY 10010

Cover design by Douglas Design Associates, New York, NY

Page composition/typography by SR Desktop Services, Ridge, NY

ISBN: 1-58115-074-1

Library of Congress Cataloging-in-Publication Data
Herbert, Katherine Atwell.
    Writing scripts Hollywood will love / by Katherine Atwell Herbert.—Rev. ed.
        p.   cm.
    Includes bibliographical references and index.
    ISBN 1-58115-074-1
    1. Motion picture authorship.   2. Television authorship.   I. Title.
PN1996.H43   2000
808.2'3—dc21   00-045407

Printed in Canada

Contents

INTRODUCTION

Television, newspapers, and magazines love to tell stories about actors and directors, about current movies, and about Hollywood, where all the action happens. The important thing for writers to remember is that the process of making movies, which makes stars, which makes media attention, begins with screenplays. This pattern hasn't changed since the first edition of this book was published.

The Internet seems—at least temporarily, we have to wait for the future to see how it ultimately plays out—to have opened up the possibilities for independent filmmakers. There may be a day when moviemaking is no longer dependent on Hollywood studios for the production and distribution of movies, but that may be a bit of a far-fetched scenario. Movies will continue to be an expensive undertaking. Then, too, simply posting something on the Net doesn't necessarily guarantee anyone will watch. Isn't an audience a necessary component of art, especially the dramatic arts?

Another question to consider while being pummeled by all the Net hype is this: Just because someone has access to the means of making films, it doesn't necessarily follow that the person possesses the talent or ability to make watchable fare. When Brownie cameras became available to anyone with the purchase price, not everyone became a master photographer. Ditto with the old 8mm camera and the camcorder. Why would anyone assume the availability of digital cameras and Web sites will reverse the pattern?

Large companies, especially those businesses that already have the means to produce high-quality, big-budget productions, may move their operations exclusively to the Internet when and if that seems to be the best way to continue operating the company and making a profit. If that happens, the process of selling a script may change—it may all be done online, for example, but there will still be the need to evaluate incoming material in an effort to find projects that are worth developing. Meanwhile, until that particular version of the future arrives (if it does), the game continues to be played as it has been for the past few decades.

For now, the Internet can help the novice screenwriter keep abreast of the industry and locate filmmakers and production companies. But you have to remember that although the Net gives us the feeling that we're all sitting around a communal computer as if it were some sort of campfire, there's no reason to believe a company will be any more inclined to answer your script pitch made via e-mail than they answer your telephone calls. Nor is there a guarantee that just because they'll receive your screenplay electronically rather than through the mail that they'll be any more impressed with the material.

So this second edition of *Writing Scripts Hollywood Will Love*, like its predecessor, covers all the ground aspiring screenwriters need to plow through to prevail against incredible competition and get the thumbs-up sign from the people who have the means and ability to make movies. Unlike the dozens of interchangeable how-to scriptwriting manuals, this book aims to arm the writer with information about the Hollywood process and describe those elements that are part and parcel of salable screenplays.

Opening with a reality check, the book details how the writing game really operates and reminds readers that Hollywood scriptwriting is very much a commercial enterprise. Those with artistic pretensions and ideological axes to grind, but a lack of writing craft, need not apply.

The first section ends with an explanation of the pivotal role script analysts play in a script's initial evaluation and reassures the writer that analysts are people who love to be told a good story. They want to like the script as much as the writers want it to be liked.

The chapters entitled "Building Plans," "The Simple," "The Intermediate," and "The Complicated" provide dozens and dozens of tips for creating a script that can compete with the best of those that stream into studios. Starting with suggestions on basic approaches to structure, the book then moves into ways to give a professional look to a script's visual presentation. The third chapter in this section details how the dozens of conventions that good scripts adhere to need to be incorporated into the writer's work. The final part of this section discusses the more complicated elements of discovering workable premises, things to remember when developing a plot, and suggestions for making characters come alive on the page.

Topping off the volume are encouraging suggestions to help writers keep their perspective and their sanity while they work towards success, and a series of six interviews with working producers and writers who know the business from all sides.

The advice collected for this volume comes from a great variety of professional story analysts who have collectively read upwards of 100,000 scripts at the various major studios, production companies, networks, and cable outlets. As the studios' and production companies' first line in appraising screenplays that are received, these experts have seen every script problem there is and know what elements well-crafted scripts incorporate.

Struggling screenwriters need every byte of information available to fill their arsenal of strategies, knowledge, and pluck to succeed in a very tough game. *Writing Scripts Hollywood Will Love* hopes to provide a large share of this.

* * * * *

The author has worked as a script analyst for various studios, including Fox, TNT, Lightstorm, and Viacom-Showtime. As an analyst—or reader, as the studios informally refer to them—and a development person, Atwell Herbert has been on the front lines in the battle to find screenplays worth producing. In the trenches she quickly learned the common script problems to which writers fall prey.

As a writer who has penned scripts, script rewrites, national magazine articles, newspaper articles, and film reviews, she knows the problems and pleasures writers face. Atwell Herbert is currently the Coordinator of the Motion Picture/Television Program at Scottsdale Community College in Scottsdale, Arizona. She continues to analyze screenplays.

A Pep Talk and Then Some

1

*"Fat, drunk and stupid is no way to go through life, son."**

Are you fit? Gotten yourself toned and muscled to perfection? You better be. Psychologically and physically, you've got a big job in front of you. Better to be prepared than to come up an eighty-pound weakling writer.

You probably bought this book because you're going to write scripts, or you already have and you're looking for some direction, some inside information about how it all works, and some suggestions to increase your chances of selling one.

Unlike *other* books that want you to believe that writing and selling scripts is as easy as sitting down at your word processor, this one isn't going to fool you. The doors to writing success in the film business are heavier than the Gates of Paradise and nearly impossible to crack open wide enough even for the insertion of a slim script. So, you must pump up your enthusiasm and brush up on skills to improve your chances of success. There's a phrase often heard around Hollywood: "If success in the entertainment business were easy, everyone would be doing it." Opening those doors is going to be a challenge, so let's go.

The difficult task of making your work salable is the one aspect of this career that's invariably skipped over by well-wishers, your biggest fans, college teachers, and writing mentors. Every college film/English department should include a "marketing your own writing" class that

---

*See appendix D.

would be required if a student signs up for any kind of professional writing class. Every writing workshop should include a section on making your project salable.

Most teachers, with the safety of their tenure and regular paycheck, seem to be unaware of, or choose to ignore, the highly competitive nature of commercial writing. These instructors, whether encouraging or discouraging their students, omit or skim over discussions of strategies or suggestions for getting a script sold.

One view assumes that the school's task is to train the student in writing skills, but learning the harsh realities of selling written material is up to the student. The cynic, however, believes teachers neglect the marketing aspects of writing because they're simply unaware of how it's done. Instead, the cynic wonders if the teachers actually believe the romantic tales of great literary geniuses sitting in their garrets getting discovered.

The end result of this academic omission is that students often think they're the next Quentin Tarantino, Steven Spielberg, or Alfred Hitchcock and assume that, like magic, they will be discovered.

You may want to conduct a reality check. To begin, you must know, whether you admit it or not, that thousands and thousands of people you share this country with are scribbling words on blank pages. All of them figure they are geniuses and their words are pure, explosive, and golden.

Unfortunately, there simply aren't that many geniuses. There's a very, very good chance you aren't among that rare species. (But so what, being one didn't help Van Gogh, Mozart, or James Joyce get the recognition they deserved during their lives.) It could be that you're merely brilliant or extremely gifted. The good news is this: It doesn't matter. Remember Thomas Edison's words: "Genius is 99 percent scut work." (Well, he said something close to that.) At any I.Q. level, you have to learn how to refine your craft and art, and then figure out how to present it so the world can recognize it. (Unless you want to pull an Emily Dickinson and write without any thought of selling; then you don't need this book.) But if you want to get discovered, you have to learn how to go about being *found*. And if your goal is simply to make a living as a screenwriter, you still have to learn how to go about being *found*. Remember, studio executives aren't knocking on garret doors these days.

One big step you can take toward getting discovered is making sure that your script is in the most refined and most professional state possible. Once you've put it in the mail, it's out of your hands. You don't have a chance to fix anything or explain that you planned another rewrite or promise you'll get your printer cleaned and deliver a better, more readable copy. Once your script tumbles into a mailbox, it's too late for any of that.

You wrote the script. That was difficult enough. But that was only the first half of the process. Getting your work from your desk drawer to the local neighborhood theater, the second half of the process, is more difficult. And it's the part over which both new and established writers have little control. Therefore, you must take charge of those aspects that your actions can influence. This book aims to help you gain some control by describing and clarifying those elements that are present in professional, commercial scripts, and to avoid those pitfalls that will mark your work as amateur and cause it to be dismissed from consideration and thrown in the "pass" pile. Got those biceps toned? Are you shaped up? Are you ready to be *found?*

RULES OF THE GAME 2

"If you want to be a duchess, be a duchess.
If you want to make love, hats off."

Stop for a minute here. Before you even pick up your script, there may be another attitudinal roadblock that needs to be adjusted before we go any farther. If it's not resolved, everything else in this book will be of no use to you.

CAN YOU DRAW THIS?

Some writers may lament that the movies aren't art, they're not wrought with any noble or urgent intent, they don't strive for any commendable goal. Films exist only to make money. They're probably right, at least part of the time. Those same writers might also complain that there are too many movies that numb the mind, pander to our baser instincts, or are just downright idiotic. These misgivings may often be valid, and they aren't entirely off base.

We've all heard the terms "commercial" and "fine" artist, as if there were some unbridgeable distinction between those who set up their drafting boards in an ad agency or a magazine office and those who daub their paints on canvas in a private studio. The distinction in the quality of the work between these two forms of the same profession exists only in some textbook or on some college campus where people apparently aren't concerned about paying the rent. In real life, artists often cross over between the two. They might take temporary jobs and later work on personal projects; or do commercial work during the day, but spend nights completing their masterpieces; or they may fulfill their talents by creating unforgettable and distinctive magazine covers, advertisements, or billboards.

Norman Rockwell deprecated his immense success as a magazine illustrator, while aching to achieve respect as a serious artist. Alexander Liberman has a reputation as a "fine" artist through such work as his Circle Paintings, but he also oversaw the design of all the Conde Nast publications—a commercial endeavor whose goal is to sell magazines. Ansel Adams worked for years as a catalog photographer before he ever shot those enduring, majestic pictures of the Southwest. Lastly, don't forget that Michelangelo was hired by the pope to do something with that damn ceiling.

Similarly, writers sometimes are categorized as "serious" or commercial. Yet, a corporate financial writer by day may hunker down to the word processor by night and eventually become a successful screenwriter. Some writers take on teaching or reviewing jobs so they have time to write their own masterpieces, and some copywriters or journalists actualize their talent by doing the work they are paid for, period. Jim Lehrer, the longtime PBS News Hour anchor, is like many other journalists. He doesn't just write news. He is also the author of over half a dozen novels.

Quality of form can be achieved in both commercial and noncommercial settings. What matters is the work's *merit*. How can a work, written only to sell something, be as worthy, true, or deserving of our serious consideration as a tract of prose whose intent has nothing to do with selling a product? Like it or not, the interdependence of commercial and noncommercial writing is evident everywhere you turn. For example, a sportswriter doesn't consider his writing to be commercial, i.e., he's not selling hockey sticks, he's only reporting on the game. Yet, if his editor thinks his prose is lifeless or if subscribers don't read his stories, that writer could soon be looking for a new job, because his writing ultimately must help sell newspapers. So, in a sense, he's selling a product. Now, although the writer isn't working in the newspaper's advertising department composing promotional copy, his writing is the product—and it must sell.

In the same manner, writers put their hearts into writing a screenplay and hope their work has quality and merit—that it's about or says something important. But writers must recognize that like the news scribe, their writings are also products, and they also have to be salable—to editors, to publishers, and to producers. (Unless, of course, the writer lives on government grants, is unconcerned about selling his work to anyone, and doesn't care whether anyone ever sees what he has done.) As a screenwriter, your work must attract the interest of either a producer, an agent, an actor with enough stature to get projects made, or the admissions board of a film school.

Journalists are hired by newspapers to attract readers, anchorpeople are hired to attract viewers, publishers buy books they think will sell, and movie producers buy scripts they hope will do well at the box office. This ushers in yet another twist that intertwines commercial and fine art. After you've "sold" your product—i.e., convinced a producer to read your script—that script must convince the producer that it will appeal to the public, or at least an important section of it. Or the producer must see the work as so revolutionary that it will change the course of the medium, as, say, the Armory Show changed the course of modern art in the United States. Even if a producer falls in love with a noncommercial screenplay, he has to consider seriously the consequences of bringing such a product to the screen.

With up-front costs anywhere from one to more than 120 million dollars, the necessity for commercial success is more urgent in the film industry than in most others. No one has 10 million dollars to throw away on a 120-page script with an unfathomable story, no noticeable structure, and dialogue that is unfaithful to human speech. In an industry that's an uneasy blend of art and commerce, commerce, for practical reasons, is usually the winner where there's a dispute between the two.

The point of all the foregoing is to clarify beyond any doubt that writing scripts for movies and television is a commercial craft (that's not bad, almost all writing is commercial at some level), and you need to be clear on that before you even type the title of your first screenplay—especially if you're of a mind that movies need more arty material.

It doesn't mean you tuck your heart away and run off somewhere to learn the magic formula, acquire a ruthless attitude, and go for the bucks. It doesn't mean that at all. Within the loosely-organized business that produces feature films, television shows, and movies of the week, there are lots of different options and opportunities for writers of all stripes to fit in.

Although no one in Hollywood would even whisper that the movie they're working on is arty—the word is generally eschewed as indicative of an effete or academic sensibility with no connection to how real-life working craftsmen create art, and the term signals images of artists who are too conscious of themselves being artists to produce anything valid or honest—there are films made that hope to be something besides a box office blockbuster. They're not necessarily arty, nor are they necessarily profound or important. But they're not the big-scale formula flicks that so many people think of as Hollywood's exclusive concern.

Miramax has made its reputation finding and distributing films that don't take what is considered the "usual" Hollywood approach. They've succeeded so well that Disney bought the company, and they now have secure financial backing to continue their efforts. Other companies, too, have their share of smaller-scale pictures that focus on something besides the box office tally. Fox is responsible for bringing *Boys Don't Cry* to movie houses, Miramax released *Little Voice*, and Columbia Tristar saw to it that *Go* got to the screen. A big budget and big names were featured in Dreamworks' rather unconventional—in blockbuster terms— *American Beauty*. There are as many companies concerned with releasing interesting, unusual movies as there are companies whose release slate includes only the tried-and-true formula flicks with seemingly little redeeming value. And since violent action films have of late taken a smaller share of box office dollars, while costume epics such as *Shakespeare in Love*, *Elizabeth*, and *Anna and the King* have proven there's an appetite for more variety, change is definitely in the air. Then, too, with the success of *The Blair Witch Project*, which was due in part to its Internet promotions, it's fairly certain that there's likely to be even more diverse products being made, with or without the blessings of the major studios.

Now, more than at any time in the recent past, it's possible for a writer to gain acceptance in Hollywood without having to write an erotic thriller or a story in which the body count is higher than that of the Civil War. What's more, there are stratifications of writers in Hollywood. Oh, yes, everyone wants to make rent money and most are in awe of the writer who can command more than a million bucks for a screenplay, but admired writers more often include those who have written films that have reputations for being good—whether or not they made a lot of money at the box office. Just notice which films consistently get nominated for Academy Awards.

So, if you're inclined to conclude that since this is a commercial enterprise, you have to swallow your personal vision and lower your standards, remember that 99 percent of the movies made, both highbrow and low, require a writer whose craft is well-honed. Within the industry, writers acquire reputations that range from thoughtful, intelligent geniuses down to mechanics who churn out exploitative schtick. Hollywood does distinguish between critically successful writers and commercially successful writers, but it's possible for both types to make a living.

Although critics may have some very precise ideas of what makes a good movie or a great movie, and they lament that more films don't meet their ideals, the film industry doesn't often heed their cries. In Hollywood, most studio people will tell you there are only two kinds of film: good and bad. This philosophy has produced such films as *Snow Falling on Cedars*, *The Matrix*, *The Truman Show*, *October Sky*, *Fight Club*, *The Other Sister*, and many, many others. The ramifications and interpretations of "good" may be many and varied. Remember, too, that it's easier and more fun to write a bad film review—there are so many more negative adjectives in the English language then there are positive ones—than to search for a dozen ways to say a film is good. Besides which, good films often work so well, it's difficult to break down their elemental parts and examine them minutely. And the critic and the editor know readership is heightened if a critic can pan a film with panache. We shouldn't forget that critics also have to sell newspapers or get ratings.

Ironically, although the number of Web sites dedicated to films has grown substantially in the past couple of years, and more Web-based film critics than ever weigh in with their opinions of new film releases, the proliferation has served to decrease the impact and importance of critical opinion in general, i.e., if everyone's a critic, then who's left to be influenced by them? And if anyone with access to the Internet can be a critic, how soon will we no longer be able to distinguish who's credible and who isn't?

Okay, we all understand that the movies are mostly about business. After all it's called the entertainment industry, not the fine arts industry, isn't it?

There are just a couple more roadblocks to decimate. You want to see the creation you sweated over realized on film. You prefer this to keeping the script safe in your dresser drawer or read only by your best friends. To achieve this, you have to be willing to sign on with the ranks of struggling writers. These are the people who strive for acceptance of their work and know that to win it, you have to get out in the market battlefield and be willing to fail dozens of times. You have to be willing to accept repeated rejection, but continue writing anyway. You have to understand that screenwriting is a highly competitive profession that doesn't operate with Lady Justice looking over anyone's shoulder. People whose writing doesn't deserve it make script sales. People whose writing is pure gold labor without success.

Everyone knows that the arts and entertainment business is risky—there are lots of noble failures. Knowing that, you have to keep selling and selling and selling your product, until eventually someone buys. Then, after a sale is finally realized, you have to accept yet another difficult actuality: The screenplay is no longer yours. It's subject to revision, rewrites, on-set and postproduction alterations. You can't do much about any of these aspects of the game of professional, commercial writing; you have to accept them as the ground rules. Remember, Michelangelo and the pope had lots of battles over that ceiling. And Shakespeare did a lot of rewriting.

INDUSTRY CLOCKWORKS 3

"Jack you're doing it wrong."

I t doesn't matter how many headlines scream about a multimillion-
dollar script sale or a first-time writer's unbelievable dream deal; it doesn't
make a bit of difference if, during filming, a movie stirs controversy or has
cinema buffs heaving in anticipation of its release; it doesn't matter who
does or doesn't star in a film or which studio releases it; it doesn't matter
if the critics consider the film the best ever; there is one constant. The
movie's success is primarily dependent on the script—pure and simple.

Now, we know that "bankable" stars are important—more for getting the film made than making a profit, and the value of big-name actors
can sometimes put a marginal film in the plus column. But it's really the
script. Leonardo DiCaprio, considered the hottest ticket around since
Titanic, didn't save *The Man in the Iron Mask* from a stifling box office.
Sharon Stone's *The Muse* didn't inspire an audience to line up at the box
office. Kevin Costner's *Message in a Bottle* went unseen by moviegoers,
and even the hyperkinetic Robin Williams couldn't get *Jakob the Liar* to
sell any tickets.

Huge promotional budgets and the appearance of actors on talk
shows can enable a film to open big, but even the biggest promotional
scheme in the world won't guarantee the film's success. The fall 1999
release, *The End of Days*, an overproduced, overpromoted film, deflated
like an unstopped balloon when it was released. The excessive dollars

spent on promotion can often enable a film to have a very profitable opening weekend, but if moviegoers aren't impressed by the story, the theaters will be empty by the second or third week. There are some exceptions, but those exceptions are not bad scripts. They're minimal scripts inflated with highly watchable elements like great stunts and effects, interesting performances, or even nostalgia, which benefited *Star Wars: Episode I, The Phantom Menace.*

The heart of it, the essential engine that runs every production, is the script—that unassuming sheaf of words slung across 120 pages of plain white twenty-pound bond. Regardless of whether it winds up a classic or a clinker, in Hollywood, the script starts every other process in motion.

As warned in chapter 1, you can't write masterpieces in your garret and expect to be discovered. Meditation, visualization, voodoo, witchcraft, or offering human sacrifice won't help. You have to get your script out there in the marketplace.

What is this process? Are you ready? You've finished your opus grande. You want to see it on screen. This is the much more difficult half of your quest. You thought the difficult part was taking your idea and forming a coherent story, but it wasn't. Now, you've got to get someone to read your script. Take heart. There are ways to reach that destination. We've got a road map.

AGENTS

Your first step probably should be to try to find an agent who's willing to read your script. There are various ways to go about this. The best method for getting your script to an agent is to have a friend who is represented by one. The friend recommends you, and the agent is already more interested in you than he is in the huge pile of scripts he has stacked next to his desk. The big agencies, e.g., ICM, William Morris, CAA, etc., won't even let you send a script to them unless you're recommended by one of their clients. You've got to try to find someone who can recommend you—a friend, a neighbor, a friend of your mother's, or any other relative with whom you're currently on speaking terms. They don't even have to be a friend. They can be an acquaintance or someone you meet at a party or a coffee shop. If they're a writer and they have an agent, ask them if you can call their agent and use their name. It's worth a try. Remember, Hollywood is a town where chutzpah is admired.

If none of this works for you, there is another way you can look for an agent. The Writers Guild West, in Beverly Hills, publishes a list of agents (see appendix A). Buy a list—they're cheap—and go through it. It will note which agencies are willing to look at new writers and which are not. Call all the appropriate agencies. Ask them if they have a staff agent that looks at new or unrepresented writers, and define what kind of writer—television or feature—you are. Some agencies specialize in sitcom writers or television drama writers. The large agencies have both types on staff. If an agency has a staff person who looks at new writers, they probably will tell you to send a query letter to that agent outlining your story and your experience as a writer. The smaller agencies that may have only one agent on staff will tell you whether they are looking for any new clients. If they are, they'll probably invite you to send your screenplay to them.

Don't underestimate these calls. What you're actually doing here is making the first pitch for your work. Before you punch in that phone number, decide what you're going to say. Write a brief script for yourself that includes all the necessary information. You will want to start with an introductory statement about looking for representation. Then you might give them just a couple of lines synopsizing the story and indicating its genre. Talk it up, brag about it a little. Don't tell them your mother loved it, but maybe tell them you've had actors read it aloud and the response was terrific, or something like that. In this brief conversation, you can often convince the agent at the other end of the line that you're a professional with a product they ought to look at. If they're convinced by your phone call or letter that your script might be worth reading, then you've just opened a door and gotten a toe inside. It's a valuable step forward in this half of your work.

One thing you should remember about these phone calls: Any institution that receives thousands of inquiries sometimes behaves as if they possess treasure that everyone wants. Since their phones are constantly ringing, they get weary and impatient, and it's obvious in their voice when they speak to you. It's a learned behavior. There are also receptionists and phone operators who are so impressed with their illusionary involvement with the entertainment VIPs who pass by their desks that they figure you're nothing but a meaningless mite in the universe. Then there are the clerks who have failed to learn anything about the company they work for and consequently haven't any idea to whom you should speak. Mostly, the larger agencies are businesslike, and because they're answering inquiries like yours so often, they give you the minimum amount of time possible. So, don't be surprised that making these phone calls isn't fun, but they have to be made. Don't take them personally. Write down your goal for each phone call, and don't let yourself stray from it because of the words of some rude, illiterate, congenital teenybopper whose only goal is to get to the beach before the sun goes down.

When you're invited, whether it's by an agent or an agent's assistant, to send a script, make sure that you have the agent's correct name and spelling and all other necessary information—department name, if it's applicable, the agency name with the correct spelling, the address, etc. Also, it's probably a good idea to learn the name of the agent's assistant. You probably will be talking only to this person throughout your contact with that agent. If you can become phone-friends, so much the better. As a former assistant to a head of production at a studio once said, "Writers don't know how much I can help or hinder their dealings with my boss. If they did, the arrogant ones who call would be a little friendlier." There is another saying in Hollywood: "Be kind to assistants. Next year, they may be sitting in their boss's seat." Always keep these two pieces of advice in your mind when making your calls.

There is one more piece of information you ought to know about agent's assistants: Since so many people want to work in the industry, there are plenty of talented people to choose from. Agent's assistants, who almost without exception want to become agents, in some cases already have a law degree. Nearly every assistant of any kind in Hollywood has at least one B.A. tucked in his or her portfolio. So, it's probably not smart to talk to them as you might occasionally talk to the burger flipper who can't make change for a dollar.

Follow up on all agencies that invite you to send a script or a query letter. Make a list of the companies you've called, and note the ones you've subsequently contacted by mail. After a couple of weeks, call those agencies to whom you've sent a script. If you're not interested in keeping track of your script, no one else will be either.

If your script has been read when you call after two weeks, that's a plus. You'll get your answer and can move on to the next step. Usually, however, nothing will have happened to your work. But your call will serve as a reminder to the agent or as an impetus for her to read the script. During this call, you'll want to remind the agent of the script's content and genre. If she hasn't read the work yet, ask her when you might call again. And then call at the time suggested—or a little sooner.

Agencies range from very organized and straightforward to those that don't seem to have a clue what it is they're doing. With the latter type, you wonder how they make any money. To wit, a writer sent two scripts to a small agency that she thought had only a single agent. The agent sent the feature script back with a note that she liked the writing, but wasn't too crazy about the story. She had passed the television script along to the agent in the office who handled TV. He would be getting back to her. Two weeks later, the writer called the TV agent. He didn't seem to have any idea what the writer was talking about, so she started from the beginning regarding the path her script had taken. He then said, "Oh yes, here it is. Give me a week to read it." She did. A week later, she called again. He again didn't have any memory of their conversation or her script, but promised to "look for it." Two weeks later it was much the same story. The writer gave up, figuring she didn't want to be represented by an agent this disorganized and forgetful.

The ideal scenario is that the agent likes your script, tells you she'll represent it, and asks you to sign an agency contract. That means she'll represent those scripts you write that she feels are worthy/salable for the term of the contract. It means she's serious about you, and she'll probably do some work for you. She sees promise in your writing. This kind of arrangement is rare for new writers.

The second best thing that can happen is that an agent will like the project you've sent her and agree to represent it for a specified period of time. It is more likely that an agent will tell you verbally that she likes your script, and then get very vague about it. She won't mention a contract.

When you actually talk to an agent who's interested in your writing, it's almost guaranteed that she'll ask you what else you've written (although you've sent her a brief résumé of your writing) and what you're currently working on. Don't ever admit that you're not writing anything. Agents need to be convinced that you're a working professional writer who's in this for the long haul.

Once an agent is interested in what you've written and agrees to represent you, you can't relax. Some agents are serious and hardworking—they don't take on clients casually, and they work for them—but don't count on it every time. It really depends on the agent. Many agree to send your work out to some producers, but whether they do or not, you don't know. Some say they'll represent you and don't do much of anything, except go to lunch and schmooze.

You don't want an agent who has dedicated her professional life to lunch and who you suspect can't read (although it is often rumored in Hollywood that a requirement for being an agent is illiteracy). But in the beginning, you probably should take whatever you can get—it's usually only temporary.

If you get an agent to take on your script, you should keep tabs on what the agent is doing or not doing for you. Discuss with her what her strategies are for marketing your work. She's supposed to be the inside person with up-to-date information on which companies are doing what. Your agent probably won't know everyone—that's hardly possible—but she should be abreast of current developments, trends, and productions. Let her know you're willing to do what you can to help the process along.

You also should learn as fast and as thoroughly as you can which production companies might be looking for a script like yours or which companies produce work that is similar to yours (i.e., an action script should be sent to those companies who make action films). You can learn this by reading the trades (see chapter 7); by purchasing the latest issue of a studio directory that lists the various production companies, their studio contracts, and a partial list of the films they've been associated with; by talking to the people you know; and by noting what companies have made the movies you see at the neighborhood theater. When you find companies that you think might be interested in the type of material you've written, ask your agent if she has considered sending your script to that company. The agent should be able to tell you whether it's appropriate to send your material to them. However, don't let it stop there. If you feel your material would be right for a particular company, but after talking to your agent you realize she doesn't seem familiar with the company, call the company yourself, tell them about your project, and ask them if you can have your agent send them the project. If they say "yes," call your agent and tell her that the company's expecting it. Make sure you give your agent all the appropriate information for their cover letter and subsequent calls. And don't stop with one company.

The point is, you don't want to become passive as soon as an agent agrees to represent you. You can't depend on your agent to do all the work for you. There are ambitious agents who will read your stuff, sign you on, and immediately work for you day in and day out—along with their other clients—but it's better if you don't count on that. Instead, continue working for yourself.

PRODUCERS

Another way to get your script into circulation is to solicit independent producers. Again, try to get in contact with these people through friends and acquaintances or through anyone you meet or work with who may know a producer. Producers who have well-established companies and contracts with studios, like Ron Howard and Jim Cameron, will insist that your script come in through an agent.

But there are producers all over the place who are looking for solid projects they can develop. Some have agreements with studios or networks and continually make movies. Some are well-established, have a good track record, and good relationships with studios or networks. Other producers have been involved in a couple of films, have some contacts, and are always looking for the screenplay that will make them rich and respected. Producers can tap private sources of financing or shop scripts to the major studios and the networks to obtain the necessary funding.

Finding independent producers isn't too hard. Most are listed in the directories and are mentioned in the trades when new deals are completed. The good thing is, independent producers will often read your material without it coming in from an agent. When you contact these producers by phone, you should follow the same approach as you follow when contacting agents.

If you decide you want to contact these producers via letter, that is also an option. Your letter shouldn't be longer than three short paragraphs. You want lots of white space on the page, so the producer knows he can read it quickly. In the first paragraph, try to sell the project. In the second, summarize the story, and in the third, summarize your background.

Producers, like agents, come in varying degrees of seriousness, professionalism, influence, and dedication. You can, therefore, expect a variety of responses when sending them material. Some will agree to read your script but never get around to it, while others will read it promptly and contact you with their response. Primarily, producers have two concerns: finding material they want to produce and finding financing for the production. Often small producers, who are usually only involved in one production at a time, will be unable to look at your work or unable to get back to you regarding it in any reasonable amount of time if they're in the middle of working on a production.

When it comes to producers, there is one notion you need to get out of your mind: You won't be submitting your precious, refined, and erudite work to some overweight, gold-chain-wearing, cigar-smoking ape who can't read. For all the laughs the stereotype causes in movies and stand-up routines, that guy probably disappeared when his gold chains turned green.

That's not to say to say there aren't some sleazoids wandering around calling themselves producers. And yes, there are producers in Hollywood who don't know one end of a camera or a script from another, but most of these guys don't last long—just until their money runs out. Despite what they say on the phone, or after you've called to check on the status of your script, they probably won't ever read your script, and it will take a 9.9 earthquake before they make your movie. If you get involved with one, you'll just have to chalk it up to experience and move on.

The other kinds of small-time producers, ones that don't have contracts with studios, usually have worked their way up from assistant directing or line producing. They're ready to take on an executive producer's job, but unless they have the keys to Fort Knox, they have to keep working themselves to make ends meet. Their efforts at producing are usually part-time. Nonetheless, they, too, are looking for the brass ring that they can turn into gold.

ALTERNATIVES
The Internet. It's a magic word that conjures up images of dread, of fortunes made, money lost, the future, unimaginable promise, and damnable mechanics to be struggled through, of a further democratization of society, and of an anonymity that's lamentable. The Internet, the movies, and you. Needless to say, the Net is evolving so fast that it's difficult to say anything about it or make any suggestions regarding your material and that it won't be dated by the time you read this. As a basic approach, if you're interested in getting your screenplay seen, you should check every agency, production company, and studio Web site to see if they take pitches, scripts, treatments, or synopses via the Net. Again, you need to

be sure the company makes the kind of film you've written, you need to make sure you're sending the material to the appropriate person and have their name spelled correctly, and that all the legalities—release forms, etc.—are taken care of. Also, although the Net is more casual—more like writing notes to someone rather than formal letters—I wouldn't let my e-mail messages get too chummy, too negligent of the basic rules of grammar, or too far from businesslike.

There are a couple of less-direct ways of getting your work out of the nest to see if it can fly on its own.

One route you can take to get your material out in circulation is the screenplay contests that seem to abound, and new ones crop up every year. Entering these competitions is easy. You need a good, clean copy of your screenplay and the entry fee. Winners are usually promised a cash prize, ranging from $250 to $5,000, with a few contests offering larger cash rewards. Also included as part of the payoff to the winners is an introduction to a Hollywood agent. Whatever happens after that is usually between the agent and the writers. You've got to remember, depending on the competition—there are some writer's competitions that make no impact on Hollywood—you'll be "hot" for a couple of months, give or take a month or two. It's important that during this time you run as hard and as fast as you can to make contacts, get your script placed with a company that will actually produce it, and make your agent believe you're the best thing to happen to her since William Goldman, Herman Mankeweicz, and Robert Towne rolled into one.

If nothing much comes from winning the award—say it's a smaller or less-well-connected event, and meeting with an agent never happens or you're brushed off by the one you've been introduced to—you can still use your prize as leverage. When calling agents, mentioning that you've won, or placed, in a script competition will probably make the agent sit up a little straighter in the chair and be more amenable to reading your work.

Sometimes film festivals focus on finished films, but accept screenplays as well. It's probably a good idea to check out the festivals—which you can find on the Net—and see which ones also look at screenplays.

ALTERNATIVES THAT REQUIRE A PARTICULAR FLAIR

There is a fourth alternative method of getting your scripts in front of someone's eyes. Well, it's not one way. This avenue is really lots of ways, depending on your creativity. If you don't shrink from risky games and can bluff your way through tough situations, the Shameless Stratagem method may be the technique for you. In this approach, your creativity is your salvation or your damnation.

Pose as a messenger and deliver your script to a top agent. Get the home address of an important producer or actor, dress as a pizza delivery person, and deliver your script instead of a large one with anchovies. Frequent the places where producers and agents hang out, and button-hole whomever you think is appropriate. Send an agent a series of notes touting your screenplay. Treat your screenplay like a Saturday serial and send a little at a time to a producer.

Use your imagination and come up with your own ideas. If the two conventional routes don't appeal to you or don't work out, you can try the Stratagem. There is something to keep in mind. This approach isn't for the faint of heart or faint of pride. You may be embarrassed. You may be ignored or treated like you are crazy. You may be brushed off like a dried spot on a lapel. But there's always the chance that you may intrigue someone and get him to look seriously at your script. And if it works out, you've already got a good start on acquiring an interesting reputation, a plus for anyone on the creative side of this business.

Meet the Fates

4

"I got a one-way ticket to Palookaville."

Once your script gets inside the doors of an agency, a production company, or a studio, you're at the threshold of the second and most pivotal step in your quest. It is here that your script will get its first, and maybe only, consideration and ultimate judgment at that company. That consideration and judgment comes, in almost every case, from a script analyst, or reader. These people are the ones who analyze your script from cover to cover. This may be the only time your work gets read and thought about at the company you've chosen to send it to. It is upon their experiences and insights that the material for this book of suggestions and tips was developed—because they see your work first and determine its future, or whether it even has a future, at the company they read for.

Before we explore the specific ways to make your script pass this pivotal test, it's appropriate to examine this route and the people along the way who will be considering, evaluating, and ultimately judging your material. It doesn't matter whether a screenplay or teleplay is submitted by a heavy hitter from a top agency or forced through the door by a struggling writer, you can be sure that every script in Hollywood—the big deal and the small—that becomes a major motion picture playing in a theater near you follows this same route.

Agencies and production companies receive anywhere from none or a couple of scripts—depending on how small the company is—to dozens each day. The studios and major production companies, which only accept scripts from agents, also receive maybe a hundred or so a week. The flow of scripts varies so much it's difficult to put a hard and fast number on it, but all in all, it probably averages over seventy-five a week at a studio.

After the mail's opened or the delivery person has made his drop, the scripts are logged in. This is done so the studio, production company, or agency can track them. It may not be done at small agencies or production companies—which partly accounts for why you may never get one returned in the mail, nor will they be able to find it if you call.

Sometimes particular executives and producers are waiting for a script that they're expecting from an agent—after an agent's pitched the project over the phone and gotten the okay to send it in. It may also be that other companies are alerted to the script, and there may be bidding on it. Or an agent may have opened bidding on a project by contacting all the major production companies simultaneously. If either of these is the case, the script is given the rush treatment. The executives or producers will probably read the script concurrently with the analyst. Everyone, in this case, works against a tight time restraint, and all the necessary forces are pulled together to determine and plan the company's action. This is almost the only time executives get in on the reading of scripts this early in the game.

At the next level, a script may not be generating as much heat as the scenario described above, but nonetheless, the work is from an established writer, or maybe it's part of a package that includes an agency, production company, actor, writer, and director. This material is often also considered rush, although the executives may not read the material until after the reader finishes and reports his impressions.

The next step down in this process is the regard accorded material that is the work of a well-established professional writer with good credits, but whose project isn't set up with any production company and doesn't have any prominent actors or directors attached. The story editor generally assigns the script to be read immediately or overnight by a script analyst.

More commonly, scripts come in from an agent without any fanfare or attachments. These scripts will be treated routinely. The story editor checks them in and puts them on a stack of scripts to be read. Analysts pick up the scripts, read them, and write their reports without undo hurry.

In the case of agencies, it's slightly different. At a large agency, where a new writer has to be recommended by an existing client, the material comes to the agent and is sent to the story editor to be assigned to an analyst. At agencies that have a staff member assigned to review new writers, material—received at the invitation of the agent—will come into that person's office. If the agency uses readers, the material will be given to one of them for review. If the agency is small, the agent or the agent's assistant will probably read the material. This holds true for small production companies also, although at some production companies based on studio lots, the material is covered by the story analysts working for the studio. Different studios handle it differently.

At the very small or one-person agencies or production companies, it pretty much depends on the person who runs the business. If you've convinced them on the phone to take a look at your work, they may do so immediately, or they may never get around to it. You should probably start calling them after two or three weeks. That way, they'll know you're interested, like a good salesman, and you're not just a passive cog to be ignored forever. Your script probably won't have been read when you call, although there are exceptions.

Often scripts submitted to various-sized agencies and productions companies are read promptly, but then the coverage (the reader's analysis of the work), especially if the reader recommends that the executive take a look at the script, sits on that executive's desk for some time. You should call back in a couple more weeks to keep tracking it. If you continue to get vague answers and no one can even tell you if it's been read, well, you have to decide how long you want to pursue it before considering it a dead issue with that particular company.

The process here can stretch on for weeks and weeks, although the coverage may have been assigned and completed within the first two weeks. Executives, like the rest of us, have twenty-four hours a day, but between shepherding their current projects—which usually involves a multitude of daily problems; answering the long list of telephone calls from agents, people looking for work, the crew of the current projects, and industry contacts; and keeping up with ongoing developments in the industry that might generate future projects or offer sources of financing; etc.—reading coverage or even a script often takes a back seat. In the larger companies, after positive coverage comes in, executives often read the material on the weekend. Producers and story executives are famous for toting home bags of scripts for their "weekend read."

There are times when producers are already sold on a project—generally a project they've had a hand in developing somewhere along the line—and ask a reader to do an analysis so they can get another point of view. In these cases, even if the analyst doesn't find promise in the script, the producer will probably go ahead with it. But the reader's input has been sought so the producer has another perspective on the material's assets and failings.

Invariably, someone is going to read your script before it goes any farther in the process. Well, there may be an exception or two. Rumor has it that agents sometimes don't read entire scripts, or they only scan them, or they just read dialogue, or they just read descriptions. These stories circulate, and some may even be true. You can, however, count on one thing: The script's going to be judged as a written work that must be cinematic.

Despite any rumors to the contrary, in most cases, an analyst will read your script to evaluate it and judge its possibilities as a film. Usually, the analyst's evaluation is the only one you'll get at the company the analyst works for. If the analyst says "pass," your script's going to go no farther.

PICKING SCRIPTS APART

Like every other aspect of the business, analysts come in all varieties. There are no particular credentials required. At small agencies or production companies, the agent or producer may read your material. Or they may have their latest assistant, who could be anything from a bimbo to a Ph.D., read it. But more often, your material will be read by people who make their living as script analysts, have been doing it awhile, and consider themselves professionals.

Since script analysts have a life-or-death power with regard to your work, at least at the company they work for, you ought to know something about them.

An analyst, or reader, is part of a nearly-invisible force in Hollywood. They are workers who don't have power lunches with big-time producers or stars, who don't carry their cell phone with them at all times, who don't call their agents daily, and whose pay doesn't rate headlines. Mostly readers sit in silent offices working through a stack of scripts and turning in their reports. Or in the case of freelancers—the majority of analysts in town—they sit at home in an easy chair or at a desk or lying in bed at any time of day or night reading through a stack of scripts, writing their evaluations, and hauling them into the office the next day. Every month, thousands of scripts get churned through the business in just this manner. The process isn't glamorous, box office idols aren't included, financial scandals don't arise here, it doesn't get covered by the E! Channel, and few people outside the business know how it works, but it's the way of the film industry.

As with every other area of the entertainment industry, there is a Readers Guild (which recently merged with the Editors Guild). Any company that is a signatory to the International Alliance of Theatrical and Stage Employees (IATSE) contracts must employ only union readers. This includes primarily the major studios. The union roster is made up of nearly three hundred readers, over two-thirds of whom are employed on a regular basis. The union assures members an equitable pay scale and first chance at openings at signatory companies. Readers must work for a signatory company for a period of thirty days before they can apply for membership in the Guild. Yes, I'm sure you see the Catch 22 here.

Experienced professional readers fill the Guild's roster. People who get into the Guild are freelance readers with lots of experience. Additionally, at any time, thirty or forty members of the. Guild are on inactive status, since they're working in management positions, have retired, or have withdrawn to pursue writing projects.

As explained earlier, there is lots of talent to choose from in the business, so lots of educated, well-qualified people fill all sorts of jobs. All the analysts interviewed for this book had at least bachelor's degrees; many had graduate degrees besides. Of the approximately one thousand script analysts working at the studios or full- or part-time freelance, most have college credentials. With a couple of exceptions, the analysts consulted for this book held degrees in the fields of English, film, or communication.

Although the industry is too often accused of being a "boys' game," in the area of script analysis, the field's pretty evenly divided between men and women. The age of analysts also runs the gamut, from people in their early twenties, still studying at U.C.L.A. or U.S.C. film schools, to experienced hands who've been with one company or another for fifteen or twenty years.

A majority of the readers employed in Hollywood aren't in the union. For the most part, they, too, are experienced professionals who make their living reading scripts. Some readers choose not to be in the

Guild, some see no advantage for their particular career goals, and some haven't yet had the chance to join.

Although readers are a pretty diverse lot, the ones interviewed for this book fall into one of two camps concerning their careers. Many are published or produced writers and hope to continue to pursue goals in the writing field, as well as continue to read scripts. Others see script analysis as a rung up the ladder on the creative side of the business. From here, they may hope to become a story editor, creative director, production or story executive, and maybe eventually a vice president of production. A minority of script analysts consider reading a permanent career, but there are those who find fulfillment in it and plan to stay.

Despite their various career objectives and general diversity, script analysts are pretty much in agreement when it comes to their work. Not surprisingly, the most common trait shared by those surveyed is their love of movies, especially good movies, and their love of the process called Hollywood. What they want is to see lots more good movies during their lifetimes, hence, they're always looking for good scripts.

Another characteristic all analysts share is a love of reading. That's probably why they've gravitated to this job. They have always been good readers and have always enjoyed it. It's second nature to them. Like a child, every reader wants to be told a good story with characters that come alive. Analysts hope every script is a real page-turner. Additionally, unlike the ordinary reader, the script analyst must be able to imagine the story on the screen.

BEGIN WITH "FADE IN"

When your screenplay reaches that pile of scripts waiting to be read, what will happen to it?

Many analysts, especially freelance readers, have little choice. They're given a script or a stack of scripts to read, and that's that. At studios, readers take scripts off the pile. A reader at Warner Bros. said, "I just take the first script off the top of the stack." Another analyst at Warner's said, "If there are no priority scripts and I have a choice, I sometimes flip through scripts to get an idea of what they may be about before I choose one to read."

Lots of readers look first at the heft of the script they're about to read. As one analyst said, "I look at the length. If it's over 150 pages and the script hasn't been advertised as an epic, my assumption is that the writer doesn't know how to tell a story in the context of film."

Nearly all script analysts also look at a screenplay's length as the first or second step when they get a reading assignment. They want to see if it falls within the standard script parameters of 100 to 130 pages. If it doesn't, the reader will wonder about the writer's professionalism. Readers also look at the page count to estimate the amount of time it will take to read the work, since in the case of freelancers, the number of scripts they read determines the amount they get paid.

Some readers look at the title. A senior vice president at a small, well-known independent production company said, "I start by looking at the title page to see if it's clever and to see its presentation. If there's a typo, that's a problem. If the title is hackneyed, that's a problem." Chris Meindl, a reader formerly with MGM, also points out the importance of that first look at the title, "Titles are sometimes an indication that the writer has given this project more than a moment's thought. Good titles will have resonance or call up associations. Too many scripts have two-word titles that sum up a high-concept story, and we already know how the story works before we even read it."

At this point, a small judgment about your script has already been made. But it's not over. Even if the title is clichéd or uninspired, even if there's a typo on that first page, most readers, like one at a major studio, "always feel excited and up about starting a new script."

Analysts immediately gain many more impressions as they begin to read. Ted Dodd, a story analyst at Columbia who also teaches at U.C.L.A. film school, hopes that there's nothing to notice in the first few pages. "As long as a script follows proper format, I don't notice." But, he adds, "If it's hard to get started and I have to reread the first pages a couple of times, that's bothersome." Freelance analyst Laura Glendining, who reads for a major network television movie division and a major television syndicate, agrees that initially she only notices the opening pages if they're not in standard format, and she knows that "if the typeface isn't standard, it'll be a hard read."

Frank Balkin, a reader for Gimbel-Addison Productions, first notices the script's "neatness, grammar, and punctuation."

These sentiments are echoed by nearly every other reader interviewed. In short, illiteracy is a great turnoff for script analysts.

A senior vice president of production at Twentieth Century Fox is also concerned by spelling and grammar, and additionally, she's put off by scripts that "are too dense. There's not enough white space on the page."

Or, as Allan Page, a reader at Warner Bros., remarked, "A script needs to be easy on the eye. It should be script-like, rather than novelistic." Being too dense, of course, means there's too much description being written, which means that the writer is probably overwriting.

For producer Neil Russell, sloppy work is very irritating. "If I can read the first page and find no typos, I'm impressed. It's always surprising, even among professional writers, how many forget to assure that margins are uniform, pages aligned, and dialogue isn't carried from one page to the next. These things make it easier on the reader."

Another reader at Warner's feels that, "If the script features anything but a paper cover and brads, I know it's from an outside source and is probably not written by an experienced writer." David Weinstein, a former analyst, is even more to the point when he says, "It seems that the lousier the script is, the more decorated the package."

For some analysts, the first few pages of a script are indicative of its overall merit. Chris Meindl has found that "you know in the first few pages if you're in the hands of a capable writer."

Regardless of the readers' impressions after the first few pages, they will read on till the "fade out." That is the job they get paid to do, but like you, they want to enjoy their work, so they hope every script is like a day at the beach.

UNFORTUNATELY, IT'S THE TRUTH

Readers, whose daily lives are filled with reading scripts, find that writers make the same mistakes over and over. The most common errors they find in scripts, errors that persuade them the script isn't worth their company's investment, come in two areas.

For a ten-year veteran at Warner Bros., the most common script problem is "predictable people relying on clichéd events." In these scripts, she adds, "you know what's going to happen in the story after only a couple of pages." She hardly needs to read further, but of course, she does. Being bereft of any surprises or unusual story turns and twists, she has to force herself to turn the pages of a script, rather than anticipating what's to come.

Robin Campbell, a freelance reader, finds too many scripts in which the writer has expressed no original voice, but instead "thinks in terms of movies they've already seen." It is just that particular writer's version of a Quentin Tarantino movie or another visual-effects-laden fantasy inspired by video games, or whatever genre is generating interest at the box office.

The lack of interesting, nonstereotypical characters is the most common problem found by readers. For David Weinstein, writers too often forget characterization. In too many scripts, "there is none," he said. Another analyst agrees that the story's characters often sink a script, but he's more concerned that too many writers create "characters we don't care about."

Nonetheless, the readers stick with it to the end and turn each page, hoping to find originality, something unusual that will spark their interest, a creative approach to the plot development, the hero's problem, the description of characters, and the theme. Most of the time, they don't find it.

When readers finish reading, their next chore is to write the coverage of the script. This involves three parts.

The first section of the coverage form generally includes the basic information on the script: the title, the writer, the agency representing it, the genre, the time period, the length, and such information as that. There's some variation among studios, but not too much. Individual elements of the script get box scores. The items that are rated here normally include: premise, story line, characterization, structure, and dialogue. They are usually rated: excellent, good, fair, or poor. The crucial item in the first part is whether the reader recommends the script, passes on the script, or thinks it should at least be given a second look. Usually, the reader can add an addendum if he thinks the script deserves a second look. Other studios give four choices: pass, not recommend, consider, and recommend. All companies have variations of these options when they use readers to evaluate the scripts they receive.

The second section of the reader's report is the synopsis of the story. As you already guessed, the reader writes something akin to a book report. Different studios have different requirements here also. Some like them very long, two pages double-spaced or maybe single-spaced, while others prefer four or five paragraphs on any story they get.

Writing comments is the final part of the reader's work. It is here that the analyst will discuss what she sees as the story's essential strengths and weaknesses with regard to the screenplay's premise, story line, characterization, structure, and dialogue. Some readers also have to include the commercial possibilities of the work, while others leave this aspect to producers, limiting their input to the value of the work as a cinematic tale.

Because they read scripts day in and day out, analysts see just about every story imaginable—although they find too many that resemble each other. In the end, they only remember the ones that were distinctive. Unfortunately, the distinctive ones seem to make up a small minority of all the scripts coming into studios and production companies.

With the great numbers of scripts they read, readers estimate any-where from 5 to 30 percent can be characterized as "good." Laura Glendining estimates that "about 40 percent of the scripts I read are com-petent." Chris Meindl is surprised "at how many good scripts I read, and I'm disheartened to watch them disappear into obscurity when a place should have been made for them." Kim O'Hanneson, a reader at Paramount, agrees that about 25 percent of the screenplays she reads are worth a second look.

If the reader recommends that the studio or company pass on the project, i.e., turn it down, the project usually stops its forward motion at that particular venue. The analysis, along with the script, is returned to the producer who brought the project in or accepted the material from an agent. The producer reads the coverage and, in most cases, accepts the reader's recommendation and returns the script to the agent or writer. The producer may still find something in the coverage that, although the script's not endorsed, might be commercial. Then, the producer may go ahead with the project despite the reader's pass. It doesn't happen often. Usually, if the producer retains any interest in a project after reading cov-erage that recommends a pass, or if the work is the product of a writer the producer admires or has obligations to, he might assign another analyst to the project. If this happens, the script gets a second chance at impress-ing an analyst. Generally, however, this second read confirms the first reader's recommendation, and the script is ultimately rejected.

If an agent has sent the script to the studio proper, and not to a particular producer, and the reader passes on it, the materials go back to the story editor (the story department staff person who oversees the flow of work) and the coverage sent to a story executive (also called a devel-opment executive, i.e., a staff person who's charged with finding and developing movie projects). If that executive agrees there is nothing in the material that sparks any interest or promises a commercially viable project, the screenplay, excluding the coverage, is returned to the agent.

If agencies turn down your project, they'll return the script to you (some smaller agencies require that you send them a self-addressed stamped envelope) with their rejection letter. They don't include the coverage.

If your script is returned, your task is to "pick yourself up, dust yourself off, and start all over again" by getting back on the phone. We've all heard the stories of writers submitting their work to dozens and dozens of producers before anyone expressed any interest.

When readers recommend that the studio or production company consider the material, your script and its coverage follow a different path. At a studio or large production company, the material and the coverage will be returned to the producer. After reading the coverage, he will decide whether they want to pursue the project any further. If they do, they start by reading the script.

The result of their reactions to your material can vary. Although the producer may agree that the material's good, he may not personally respond to it enough to pursue it. They may like the writing and will consider you for other writing assignments they may secure. They may like the idea, i.e., the premise, but remain unimpressed by the writing. In these cases, they'll either pass, buy the idea and give you story credit and then hire other writers to rewrite it, or they may like the material enough that they try to develop it. They can also offer to option the material for a set period of time, or they can buy it on the spot.

A positive response to material that comes into a studio through a story executive might encourage someone to become the material's advocate. A story executive has to like the material enough to fight for it. If that happens, the material may be under consideration—which may last forever—or it can be optioned for a set period of time. It may eventually be purchased, and then again, it can lose its luster as the battles continue and eventually be dropped.

At agencies, you hope that an agent will like the material enough to sign you on as a client. When an agent gets positive responses from analysts, they will usually read the script. Agencies and individual agents have to consider how many clients they currently represent and if they can take on another.

One way or another, your work has to impress the script analysts who will be reading it.

Remember that readers are not your enemies. They can be your advocate at the company. If they really like a piece, they write about it positively and can champion it as the process proceeds.

And although studios and production companies can only produce a small percentage of the scripts they receive, analysts want to like what you've written. They like finding good material. For heaven's sake, if you had to read all day, wouldn't you love it when you found something wonderful to read? Wouldn't you always hope that the next script was going to knock your socks off? Yes, you would, and so do analysts. They always hope to be entranced, charmed, and intrigued by what they read. When you pick up a novel, you want to get immersed in it. Readers also want to dive deep into your script and not come up until the final page. And if during the course of their read, they learn something new about a profession, an event, about history, a geographical area, or about a group of people, so much the better.

Readers want to find good scripts they can enjoy, care about, remember, and promote. They keep looking for them. Let's make sure your script is the one they love, the one they want to see play out on the big screen.

BUILDING PLANS

5

"We keep no secrets from our readers."

There's a story with a dozen variations that seems to continually go around Hollywood. Basically, it goes something like, "Well, they say there are only three story ideas" or "There are only seven basic story ideas." The numbers undoubtedly change from one day to the next and from one person to the next.

Where this thing got started is a mystery, but it's probably the result of too many people not reading enough and listening to the wrong people too much. It may also be some generalized, unconscious rationalization made by screenwriters who fear they lack imagination—if there are only seven basic ideas, then their inability to come up with something new is understandable. Maybe it's the remark of a Hollywood apologist who unknowingly defends the industry's penchant for redoing material or releasing films that are remarkably similar to successful projects already on the market. And maybe it's said in light of the knowledge that for the past century, Hollywood and every other medium has released so much material that it just seems like every story's been told, every idea mined for its story potential—whether told through film, novel, song, poem, or a non-fiction documentary of some sort—so much so that nearly anything seems clichéd, used up, and predictable.

One analyst thinks the idea of a limited number of basic stories has its origins in a confusion between premise and theme. Most basic literature classes teach that there are three basic themes: man against man, man against nature, and man against himself. Somehow this has evolved into three or seven or four story ideas. This same analyst feels that this faulty bit of lore should be replaced by something a little more useful, such as, "There's a story for every one of the seven deadly sins, and like musical notes, the combinations (of notes or sins) creates the possibility of an incredible number of stories or songs."

Whatever the origin of the concept of a limited number of stories, it's best to toss this concept (or rationalization) right out of your head.

You'll worry—what with the plethora of scripts around and the number of outlets for written and visual (filmed, digitally-created, video-taped, etc.) material growing with each new Web site, e-mail address, motion picture company, and cable outlet that is created—whether or not your material is original enough. Better you worry than to think you're the only person in the world that's written a teen angst or super-hero story. If you aren't concerned, it could mean you're not paying atten-tion to what's going on in the field in which you want to succeed. But don't despair. How can you possibly find a completely new topic about which to scribble a script? (And if you could, Hollywood would probably consider it noncommercial.) Remember your Bible? In Ecclesiastes 1:9, it says, "There is no new thing under the sun." Your screenplay probably has some very familiar elements.

GEORGES POLTI

In 1868—yes, that long ago—a fellow by the name of Georges Polti sur-veyed literature in detail and came to the conclusion that all plots fit one of thirty-six models. He wrote a book detailing his work entitled, obvi-ously enough, *The Thirty-Six Dramatic Situations*. He delineates at length the thirty-six possible story types and the elements that are necessary to successfully create each kind of story. It's kind of like he's pulled out the archetypal pattern for all the stories ever written and codified them in his book. The boilerplate, as it were. For example, he has one category enti-tled "Revolt." The elements necessary are a tyrant and a conspirator. But there are additional elements and possibilities for that particular story type. For example, the story can feature a conspiracy by one individual or by a group of people. The same elements apply if the story revolves around a revolt rather than a conspiracy. Think of *Hamlet, Braveheart,* or *Norma Rae*.

Not only does Polti about cover the gamut of story situations, his work can also serve as a guide if you get in trouble with your story by providing a discussion of the essentials of your story and the elements you perhaps forgot to include. Or he can furnish inspiration for turning an idea into a real story by offering the elements that will be necessary to include (for that story type) as you develop your premise.

Maybe someone in Hollywood at one time read Polti's book, and over the years, the story ideas got abbreviated from thirty-six situations to seven. Oh, well, no matter. When you're ready to move from idea to creating a story, you can consult Polti. Or not.

JOSEPH CAMPBELL

If you're writing screenplays, you ought to know something of Joseph Campbell's work, *The Hero with a Thousand Faces*. Just in case you're unfamiliar with Campbell, he was a professor of comparative religion who became the president of the American Society for the Study of Religion. Campbell wrote many, many books, including *The Power of Myth* and *The Masks of God*. Most of his work dealt primarily with myth and the important role it plays—and always has played—in our lives and spiritual needs and development.

Through his work, Campbell gained a certain visibility beyond the academic community. And after he appeared on Bill Moyers' *World of Ideas* show on PBS discussing his work and views of man and myth, his writings were included on many people's "must read" lists.

Meanwhile, a student at the University of Southern California, Chris Vogel, also discovered Campbell's work. It seemed to him to provide the proper analysis of the underlying story pattern—the hero's journey—he had seen, but had never been able to articulate, in hundreds of stories and screenplays he had read as a Hollywood script analyst.

So captivated by this material was he that he wrote a memo to himself about the pattern and the many screenplays that seemed to fall within its parameters. He eventually shared the memo with his coworkers and bosses, and it became known around town. Eventually, he expanded on the material and wrote a book, *The Writers Journey*. It's a storytelling aid for writers that explains in detail the twelve steps of the hero's journey. Think of *Star Wars*, *The Terminator*, or any of dozens of other films. Vogel describes how those stories work in terms of the twelve steps, beginning with a seemingly ordinary hero-protagonist who, like

Luke Skywalker, gets the call that he must respond to, and thereby begins a grand adventure full of danger, risk taking, heroism, and finally conquest of the forces that he is battling. Yes, George Lucas preceded Vogel in his discovery of Campbell. In fact, some of Bill Moyers' series of shows with Campbell were videotaped at Lucas's Skywalker Ranch.

If the hero's journey approach sounds too involved and overwhelming to you, all is not lost. It's not required that you read the book and follow the steps as if you were painting by number (Vogel didn't have that as a goal when he wrote the book). It's also not required that you toss out every plot idea you have if it doesn't seem to follow the pattern. What it does mean is that if you want to be a professional Hollywood writer, you ought to be familiar with the material, the concepts, and at least Campbell's and Vogel's names—even if you're just looking to "sound" knowledgeable at the next party you attend.

It's another way to look at story building. You can see it as a second method, following Polti's thirty-six situations, or you can see, perhaps, how Polti's situations might fit the hero's journey pattern.

ARISTOTLE

Yes, that Aristotle. That Greek guy of so, so long ago seemed to have opinions on everything, including drama and storytelling. And his opinions articulated the basic conventions of storytelling that have influenced writers throughout the ages and continue to do so even to our own time.

Aristotle created the concept that drama must adhere to the unities of time, space, and action. Further, he concluded that drama is required to have a beginning, middle, and end, and spoke of catharsis as one of the purposes of drama. Or in other words, in Hollywood terms, three acts and the feeling that a just and satisfying conclusion is reached by the end of act three. If you're unfamiliar with this concept, it's another one you should get to know. Any screenwriting manual will cover it, and most analysts in Hollywood use it as a basic tool when evaluating scripts. Essentially, the three-act structure consists of the story set-up, the complications, and the resolution, i.e., acts one, two, and three. In act one, we need to learn who your story is about and find out what sets the protagonist's story in motion. Act two is full of complications. The hero tries to solve the problem that's been introduced in act one, but runs into trouble at every turn. In this act, we find out more about the hero and the people that surround him. Act two can end when the hero thinks all is lost or all is solved. But it isn't—in either case. Act three is the resolution. It is here that everything gets sorted out.

Think of *The Fugitive*. A prominent, good-hearted doctor who's very much in love with his wife is accused and convicted of brutally murdering her. On his way to prison, the bus he's on gets into an accident and is hit by a train. He runs. It's his only chance to prove himself innocent. That's act one. It's fairly short. It "locates" the audience with regard to who the story is about, where they are, who they are, and a little bit about what they're like. It also introduces and sets up the problem to be solved during the remainder of the film. During act two, the hero's task, his goal, is clear. While keeping one step ahead of the law, in this case federal marshals, he has to find out who really killed his wife. He runs into complications; takes extraordinary risks; takes intelligent, rational steps to discover the real culprit; and finally, uncovers the murderer and the man who hired him. That's act two. Act three is a high-speed, short section that, in this particular film, is basically a chase. The hero confronts the man behind his problems, and they do battle. The hero emerges bruised and damaged, but triumphant by story's end.

The three-act structure is a good, solid basic approach to structure. Hey, it was good enough for Aristotle and hundreds who followed his tenets. The structure can accommodate Polti's and Campbell's approaches. You need to remember that throughout, there is rising tension, more is at stake as the plot unfolds, and everything should reach a point of climax and a satisfying resolution (that's the catharsis part), i.e., all the story lines are resolved in one way or another. This rising pattern is called the story arc.

ALTERNATIVES

There are those in Hollywood who feel that movies don't need to follow any of the preceding structural patterns. They feel the three-act approach may apply to stage work, but movies are too fluid, too plastic to be battened down with some artificial overlay of "acts." Movie stories run continuously from one story point to another, without those points necessarily falling into acts. Others say that even when the act breaks aren't necessary noticeable (as is only right, no one's bringing down the curtain as is done in theater), nonetheless, they're there.

Some people in Hollywood will advise screenwriters to make certain that there is a peak in the action at least every fifteen pages.

Naturally, there's a progression of the hero's efforts to solve the problem that he's been saddled with. In other words, there's still a story arc, but the tension doesn't rise and fall at set intervals (the end of each act, with the final climax coming at the end of act three), but instead, there needs to be tension and action scenes at close enough intervals to prevent the audience from becoming bored.

COMPUTER-AIDED HELP

In addition to script-formatting programs, you can also buy, sometimes as part of the script-formatting program, story aids. *Dramatica Pro* and *Movie Magic*, as well as others, offer a story-building program. Basically, these aids take you through a series of questions that assist you in creating the basic biographies of your characters and the plot points of your story. They also give you options for events you might want to have occur and story questions you'll have to answer. They're yet another method of helping you create your story, and they're generally based on the established storytelling approaches.

However you choose to approach your stories, the above methods can help. Especially if you reach page 40 or 62 or 83 and your story stalls. You've run out of material before you've reached the end of the story. Whatever your view of structure, you would do well to be familiar with the standard, accepted approaches to storytelling.

THE SIMPLE

6

"Well, that's a start."

Now that you've finished the superfast review of storytelling basics, let's move on to another important area: the script's first impression.

When your script is pulled out of its envelope, the story editor, consciously or unconsciously, decides immediately how promising it looks—based on its appearance. When the editor asks the analyst to read the script, she will probably add an editorial opinion or two about it, such as, "I hope *you* find it interesting" or "I hope *you* don't mind reading a script with a chartreuse cover and a title printed upside down." With this kind of introduction, the reader is already on the alert that the money to be made from reading the script might hardly be worth the effort.

Now, you don't want your script to get this kind of introduction, so you've got to learn how to avoid I.S.D.—instant script death.

Analysts give a script an immediate sizing-up before they read it. They look at the cover, bindings, the title page, flip through it, and check the length. To pass this first informal inspection, your screenplay must look like the most professional scripts that come across the desk.

So, pull your script or scripts out of that desk drawer and lay them on the desk while you read this chapter. Every time your script doesn't follow the current conventions, make the necessary change. After you've finished the chapter, your work should pass this first test with ease.

THE SCRIPT'S APPEARANCE

PACKAGING MAKES PERFECT

To make your script look like the ones from top writers, start with the cover. Binders should serve their purpose without calling attention to themselves. Expensively-bound scripts don't earn extra credit. Most scripts that float around the Hollywood studios are packaged in one of three kinds of covers.

The best and most common bindings are card stock—a little lighter weight than a file folder—white covers with a binding that folds inward over the three-holed script paper, thereby covering the brads (see figure 1). These covers secure the pages and protect whoever reads the script from being scratched by the brads or getting them caught on something. The bendable cover is a must for transporting and holding the script as it's read.

FIGURE 1

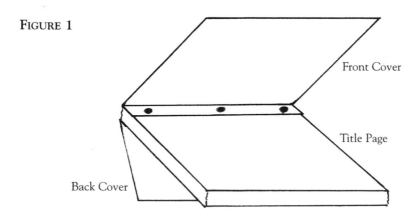

Front Cover

Title Page

Back Cover

The second most common script cover is the same heavy paper cover without the fold-over binding that covers the brads. This type also allows for ease in handling, although the reader will battle with the brads on occasion (see figure 2).

Finally, the third most common script cover is no cover at all. This is essential for shorter scripts, such as those written for half-hour or hour-long television shows. The cover of the script is simply the title page.

The primary purpose of the cover is to protect the script and hold the pages together. If there is no cover, the front and back pages may get torn off as the script is handed from one person to another at a studio or

FIGURE 2

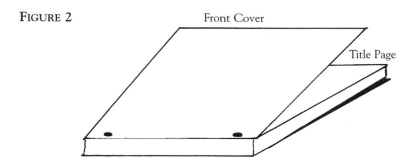

Front Cover

Title Page

production company. This isn't much of a problem with a short script, but it certainly happens to feature-length pieces.

The cover must also enable the script to be identified from its spine. Scripts are usually piled or lined up on shelves like books. Because studio personnel must be able to locate a script easily, the title is usually printed on the bound side of the pages with felt pen. If the pages are encased in a cover that makes this impossible, the script becomes a burden to the person charged with keeping track of them.

Then, too, the script's binding should never interfere with the presentation of the story. Therefore, covers are usually white, black, or anything bland. If you think it would be appropriate or clever to cover your script in a color that reflects the story's theme or message, or in a binder with a picture on it, reconsider. Analysts in Hollywood recognize this for the amateur approach that it is.

Covers need to be analyst-friendly, because those desperate devils are the people who schlep them around. They have to hold the script as they read it and flip through it repeatedly when they write their coverage. So, if the brads are secure and covered, the script probably won't fall apart while it's being handled, nor will the brads scrape across the reader's desk or turn sideways and get caught on all matter of minutiae. Also, if the cover is a neutral color, it won't distract the analysts' attention while they read it, and if it bends easily while lending a little body to the script, so much the better.

WRAP IT UP

As mentioned above, in the discussion of covers, brads are the only way to secure the pages of a script. You probably know what brads are, and if you don't, here's a picture of one (see figure 3).

FIGURE 3

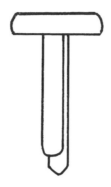

Brads win the popularity contest in script binding. Since brads can be easily removed, the script can be taken apart, copied, and then rebound. If a reader likes your script, copies are made so it can be read by more than one story executive. Even if only one executive reads the script, a copy is often made and the original filed. Using binders other than brads makes it impossible to put the script back together after copying.

An additional minor point or two need to be made about brads. Generally, although scripts are printed on three-hole paper, only two brads are used—one at the top and one at the bottom. This seems to be done more from custom than for any practical purpose, but it does save the studio a little time and the writer a teensy bit of money. Make certain that you use the proper size brads. For a standard screenplay, the 1½-inch length is a good size. If the brads used are too short for the script, the pages will fall apart before the analyst reaches the end of the first act. That will surely divert attention away from your story, and you don't want that.

LEAN AND LOVELY

After the cover, the first thing a reader notices is the script's heft. If it's fat, the reader dies a little—it will take forever to read the darn thing. Almost immediately then, the analyst wants to know the page count—this is especially true if the reader is a freelancer. Getting paid by the script means that analysts want to read as many as possible. You occasionally see a reader swoon when a script runs over 140 pages. Overweight scripts cause problems at all levels of development. Although we're currently getting assaulted with movies that run about three hours, give or take some, writers new to the game, as yet unproduced, or without an established reputation should stick to the conventional length. Yes, *The*

Green Mile, on the strength of Stephen King and Tom Hanks, ran long. *Eyes Wide Shut* and *Magnolia* did also. But they came in with impressive participants attached.

Common wisdom dictates that scripts run between 100 and 130 pages, and that's using Courier font (12 point), not Times Roman, an important distinction to remember. Currently, many script submissions run from 105 to 120 pages. This is especially true of movie-of-the-week (MOW) scripts. Be on the safe side; limit the length of your script so it will fall around 120 pages or slightly less. If your screenplay is running long (over 130 pages), you would be wise to cut it. Oh, come on, you can cut it. You just think you can't. Read it again. You'll find an unnecessary scene, a description, or dialogue that runs too long. Trim it back.

Conversely, anorexic scripts are also suspect. If your work's too thin (it runs less than 100 pages), read it through again. Are your scenes too elliptical? Will a reader glean all the information they need from them? Have you set each scene sufficiently? Does your story miss necessary beats? Check out your script, and see where a little more story needs to be told.

THE TITLE PAGE

After the analyst has given your script the once-over and made some initial judgments, the next set of impressions begins. Upon opening the cover, the first thing that comes into the reader's view, naturally, is the title page—or it should be.

TITLE

The title page contains very little information. About twenty to twenty-five lines from the top of the page, the name of your story should appear, centered and in capital letters. Sometimes the title is in boldface. It doesn't matter. Some manuals will tell you to underline the title. Underscoring is standard format for television scripts, but feature film scripts come both with and without their titles underlined.

Television scripts follow the title format above for the series name. Four to six spaces below the series title, the segment name is capitalized, centered, and put in quotation marks. It isn't generally underlined. For example, if you've written a script for *Ally McBeal,* the title would be: <u>ALLY MCBEAL</u>. The segment title appears thus: "THINGS THAT MAKE YOU GO . . ."

AUTHORSHIP NOTATION (CREDIT LINE)

Four or five spaces below the title, also centered, in upper and lower case, the author writes one of four things: "by," "Written by," "An original screenplay by," or "Screenplay by." Most scripts use the simple "by," but it doesn't matter as long as what you write conveys the necessary information without getting in the way.

YOUR BYLINE

From two to four lines below the credit line, center and type your name in appropriate upper and lower case letters.

CONTACT INFORMATION

Down at the bottom, at about line fifty-five, at either the left margin or on the far right hand side, you type your name, address (street, city, state, and zip), and phone number. And if you care to, you can also include your fax and e-mail information. If you have an agent, the agent will put her name, address, and contact number instead of yours, or in addition to yours. Putting your name, address, and phone number on the script is necessary if you're not represented by an agent. The production company has to know where they can contact you. If you put the necessary information in your cover letter, you must still put it on the script itself. It's too easy for the letter to get separated from the script, and if that happens and you haven't put your name on the script . . . Well, you can imagine the result of the oversight. Besides, the story editor often keeps the cover letter received from you or your agent. After the reader completes his coverage of your script, the story editor needs to put the two back together again.

That's it. That's all you need on the title page. In fact, you shouldn't have anything else. Oops, there are a couple of exceptions.

ADDITIONS

If you've taken your story from a novel, magazine article, or short story (that is, you own the rights or have contracted for the rights to the material), underneath your byline, you can include: "Based on the story (novel) (magazine article)," and then name the literary source. You can also include the author's name in the citation (see appendix B).

OMISSIONS

There is also information that many new writers seem compelled to include that shouldn't appear on the title page.

DATES. Don't include the date on the title page. If the script is over a few months old, the reader will figure it has made the rounds and everyone has passed on it. (Of course, it probably has made the rounds. Remember the Lawrence Kasden story? His script for *Body Heat* was supposedly turned down about seventy times before someone took a chance on it, and he already had Hollywood writing credits. It's instructive to note that he didn't go public with the rejection story until *after* the movie was a success.) You don't want your work to have a shopworn feel about it, so don't include a date.

Aside from feeling that the script has been turned down by everyone, a date that's long past makes analysts and story editors wonder if you've written anything lately. Do you have only that one work? And if not, why didn't you submit your latest project?

Third, if you send out a script that has an old date on it, readers will wonder if the story's fresh and contemporary. There are manuals that tell you to include the date you finished typing the screenplay. That advice is, if you'll pardon the expression, out-of-date.

DRAFT NUMBER. Telling story editors and analysts which draft you're sending them is also unnecessary and suggests that the writer lacks an understanding of the term "draft."

Here's the secret about draft numbers: No matter how many times you rewrite your script before you slip it in an envelope and head to the post office, it is the first draft. It will remain the first draft until you've made a deal and they ask you to rewrite it. Your rewrite, under contract, becomes the second draft (and there probably will be many others until you don't recognize your original story at all).

Including a draft number on the title page creates another minor problem for your work. When a story editor or analyst sees a draft number, they always wonder if there is a newer draft you haven't sent them. And they wonder why you're telling them you rewrote the script so many times. It really goes back to the old saw that says, pros make their jobs look easy. No one wants to know that Frank McCourt sweated over a weary computer keyboard to create all his memorable stories, or that the three tenors practice their scales for several dreary hours every day. We want to believe they do their jobs effortlessly. In the same way, although intellectually readers know that the writer has to worry over their scripts three or four times before it takes presentable form, emotionally, no one wants to know that it took all that much trouble. Everyone wants to be told a good story and feel as if the teller is making it up on the spot. Remember, too, if you had a production deal and rewrote the script but the deal fell apart, start fresh. Take off the draft number.

WGA REGISTRATION

There's one final caution about title pages: Don't include the WGA or WGAw (Writers Guild of America and Writers Guild of America west) registration number. Nobody cares if it's registered or not. Seeing the notation that it's registered stamps the script as the work of a neophyte, and a suspicious one at that.

If you think that by including the registration number the bigwigs will be impressed that you actually know about the Writers Guild registering service and hence a little of how Hollywood works, you're wrong. Professional writers in Hollywood don't put that notation on their scripts, even if they do register their work.

Most top writers don't register their scripts because 1) they have good lawyers to represent them in case they need their authorship defended, 2) the agent they use is recognized and has sent the work to various studios, so everyone in town knows who wrote the script, and 3) even if they have registered the script, they don't want to insult the studio by seeming to assume the potential producer might steal it. So, if you feel better about it, and you can't afford a good entertainment attorney, register your work, but don't include the information on the script.

Remember, contrary to the *Art Buchwald v. Paramount* case and other tales of wicked, wicked Hollywood, probably no one will want to steal your script. So many works pass through a studio, readers and story executives are lucky if they remember what they read the previous week, much less steal it.

One final note: Hollywood is always looking for good writers. If your script dramatizes the best idea to come down the freeway in a long time and is beautifully realized on the page, the studio will want to be the first one to *discover* you. Instead of ripping off your stuff, they'll probably get you on the phone, pronto.

THE OPENING PAGES

Once the title page has been turned, the analyst wants to jump into the story. Ergo, page 1 of the script should follow the title page. Some writers think they have to provide lots of supporting information to the studio. Often this information is found following the title page, or tucked into the script's final pages, or clipped to the script, or jammed in as an afterthought between the cover and the title page. Some writers send along enough information to fill a report folder. All of the information is superfluous, hardly ever read, and the mark of a novice. The writer who wants to succeed will avoid including the following material with a script.

CAST OF CHARACTERS

Including a cast of characters just isn't done. It's done in the published version of plays (but not a working draft of a new theater offering); it isn't a convention of screenplays. Including a cast list signals to the reader that you think they are too dumb to follow your characters through the story and remember who they are. Did Tolstoy include a cast of characters in *War and Peace?* No. Did *The Usual Suspects* flash pictures for us about who was who before the action got underway? No.

If, in your 120-page script, you've introduced so many characters that you're convinced the reader will be unable to remember them, then you probably have included too many. Remember, movies resemble short stories more than novels. They can't handle a multitude of complicated subplots, a vast number of characters, and the growth and change of a dozen protagonists. There simply isn't time. Films like *Airport* come the closest to succeeding at the chore, but even in these epic, lengthy stories, we don't get to know all the various characters very well. Other than the main roles, the characters are just sketched.

CASTING SUGGESTIONS

When you wrote the screenplay, perhaps you pictured a particular actor portraying your hero. Please don't tell the studio who that actor is. Maybe, just maybe, you can comment in your cover letter that your main character is the type of guy that Harrison Ford or Edward Norton could play, but go no further than this. Don't suggest who should play the role. The popular actor you see as your character probably has work commitments set for the next several years.

When a project is put on the production schedule and reaches the point where the studio is getting serious about making it, the head of production probably will have an assistant create a list of actors who might be appropriate for the role. It's a list that can range from ten to seventy-five names.

Additionally, the head of production presumably has relationships (a Hollywood term meaning "knows") with several recognized actors; he may obtain a particular actor's services rather than doing a search. The agency that brought the script to the studio may represent actors that they recommend for the role. Large agencies often "package" projects. That means they come to the studio with a package that includes the script, actors, and often a director.

If a casting director has been hired, or at least consulted, he will bring their knowledge of what actors might be good, who might be available, and whom they know.

The casting process starts from all these sources, as well as other informal methods, e.g., the head of the studio is a good buddy with a renowned "star" and asks him or her to consider the role. Or bankable actors bring a studio a script in which they want to star.

Executive decisions probably won't be influenced by your insistence that Brad Pitt play the lead in your project. What you might not realize is that a star such as Pitt may not be available for a film role until 2088 because he's committed to other films, may have vowed never to work for the company or executive who bought your script, may have no desire to play roles like the one you've written, may have decided to take a couple years off, or any of a multitude of other reasons.

If the studio is interested enough in your script to make you an offer, you can *possibly* mention your casting suggestions in one of the meetings you have with the studio honchos. Until then, concentrate on telling a good story, and skip the suggestions.

QUOTATIONS

Following the title page, some writers include a pithy statement. The material, usually a quotation, presumably has something to do with the script's theme. Quotations are nothing more than a writer's conceit. They have nothing to do with anything. A script isn't a novel; its final form isn't in print. No one but the analyst and, if the analyst likes it, a couple of story executives will ever see the quotation. So, why bother with one?

It won't be put on the screen before the story begins. If you want this wonderful piece of quoted wisdom to illuminate your theme, then get one of your characters to say it within the context of your tale. Hanging there in a no-man's land between the title page and the story, the quotation becomes an affectation. It also signals to analysts that the piece they are about to read may very well be so terribly, terribly literary that a solid, visually-based, dramatized story will never emerge.

SYNOPSIS

Much of what has been said about casts of characters can be applied to synopsizing your story. Why include a summary? Do you want anyone to read the entire work? If you include a synopsis, there is a very good chance they won't. (Except, of course, the analyst, who, as was noted earlier, may be the only one to read the thing cover to cover.) There's a base canard heard throughout Hollywood that insists studio executives don't read scripts and agents can't read. If you give these guys a synopsis, well, draw your own conclusions.

Then, too, maybe the synopsis makes the story sound boring, banal, or hackneyed. If you send it along, the story editor may immediately surmise that your script isn't the kind of material her company is looking for and return it to you unread. Perhaps your story is just a little slip of a thing, but the characters, the location, and the theme are real knockouts. If you summarize the plot, the gem you've written won't be well-represented at all. Remember, at weekly story meetings, the log line (a one- or two-sentence synopsis) of every script covered is read aloud. If the group doesn't react favorably, your script is kaput. Don't give the studio any ammunition to shoot your script down before they've had a chance to read it through to page 120.

SCENE BREAKDOWN

Not many feature film scripts received by production companies include a scene breakdown. However, some television spec scripts, especially scripts that are samples for a proposed television series, come equipped with a listing of the scenes. Usually, if a script arrives that includes a scene breakdown, you can almost bet it's come from a small production company looking for financing. The small company wants to show the larger one that preproduction preliminaries have been completed. None of this means anything to the story editor or the analysts. They will judge the script's story. It doesn't matter if preproduction work is already underway.

Scene breakdowns for television shows are done as one of the production steps after the script is bought and put into production. They aren't done by the non-staff writer. Breakdowns for feature films are done early in the production process by the unit production manager, the line producer, or the first assistant director. They are part of the shooting schedule process; they are never done by the writer.

SCREEN TITLES

Telling the reader, and ultimately the viewer, where and when the action's taking place through the use of on-screen titles is usually unnecessary.

The setting and costumes should tell the audience when the story's taking place. Occasionally, if the story hinges around something happening within a given space of time, say a bomb must be found before it explodes, then using screen titles to indicate how much time remains may be useful. In most cases, it's not necessary. Did *Grease* include a title to tell us we had returned to the early days of rock and roll? No, we didn't need it. Usually the reader or viewer will learn from the dialogue and description what is necessary to know about the dramatic time period. *Back to the Future* is another prominent example. In this story, exact minutes are crucial to the plot. But instead of intrusive on-screen titles, the filmmaker used the town-square clock.

There are occasions when titling the location of a scene on-screen saves time and has an important place in the plot. For example, if your screenplay revolves around a particular historic event by which it is influenced, you might include time and place specifics in a title at the bottom of the screen. For example, say your story's about the night that Joe proposed to Mary just when Nevada's first A-bomb test took place. Mary's so shaken by the event that although she had planned to say yes to Joe and looked forward to becoming a little housewife, she now turns him down and dedicates her life to world peace. In this case, it could be important that we know specifically what day, date, and time it is. Still, there are other ways to show us within the context of the story itself.

Use such titles sparingly. Normally, the establishing shot should tell the audience where the story is taking place and the general time period. Establishing this information can also be accomplished through dialogue and other visual cues.

PICTURES AND SKETCHES

On rare occasions, and it seems like it's always science fiction scripts, a project comes into a studio that includes pictures or sketches. These, too, are irrelevant. One of the joys of reading is getting to use our imaginations. If you have creatures, machines, or chaos that you can't describe in the body of the work, then you may be in trouble. Including drawings, even as a single introductory page at the head of the script, isn't a good idea. It's like schoolboy doodles. Besides, it will be insulting to the story's ultimate director and director of special effects. Creating the look of the film's particular sets or characters is their art and craft.

A WORD ABOUT FORMAT

When the reader gets through the twenty-second first look and comes to page 1, your script can be handicapped if your work isn't in proper format. Think of it this way: If you submit a manuscript to a book publisher, you label your chapters and proceed to write your material in paragraphs. That's it. The editors will prepare it for its final book form. Your only responsibility is to get it on the page. With film scripts, there's no middleman, no editor to make your work presentable. It's just a direct line from you to an agent or producer. One of the conventions of screenwriting is the established and accepted format. Your script should reflect this look. You want it to look like you're an experienced writer, right?

Luckily, there are now so many good script formatting programs, such as *Final Draft, Scriptware,* and others that should enable you to give your script a slick look, a professional gloss, with very little difficulty. If you're not ready to invest in one of these computer aides, check appendix B of this book, or my book, *Selling Scripts to Hollywood,* for proper formatting practices. And, oh yes, to repeat—type in Courier 12-point. It's all about timing. Scripts are figured to be about one minute of screen time for each page. So, if you type your screenplay in Times Roman and you finish at page 120, your script is actually about 135 or so pages when it's converted to Courier, and hence too long for a two-hour movie.

GENERAL NOTES

There are just a few other prohibitions that need to be dealt with before you move on to more complicated matters regarding your script. As readers wend their way through your story, they can stumble over other irritating sloppiness and unnecessary inclusions. You want to avoid these.

MAKE IT NEAT

When a production company or an agency makes copies of a script, the employee manning the machine usually doesn't give a rat's tooth about the job. They just want to get it finished, so they can continue to claw their way to the executive office. They whisk the script through the machine, put brads in it, and deliver it to the script editor. If a page or two is missing or crooked, they probably won't notice. None of this is in your control. It's just a minor glitch you have to accept. However, you should never let your script get to a production company's office in this condition. When that opus of yours hits the story person's desk, it should be as pristine as possible.

CLEAN

Each page of your script should be as white as it was when you pulled the paper out of the box. No fingerprints, no smudge marks, no jelly smears or cigarette ashes. Remember, if it's dirty, it will not only make a bad impression, it will be reproduced that way over and over and over.

GETTING STRAIGHT

When you make copies of your script, check each page to make sure the copy machine hasn't spit out pages with the copy on an angle.

READABILITY

While you're checking pages for any that may have gone astray in the machine, also make sure that the printing is dark enough to be read easily. If there are pages printed in a noticeably lighter or darker tone, you ought to go back to your original and reprint it until all the pages match. Scripts whose printing varies from page to page are irritating and, again, will pull the reader away from the content and into the form.

A final note on printing. If there's anyone out there who's still using dot matrix printers, stop! If your machine uses this printing method, have your scripts printed at a copy center with a laser printer. The dot matrix was the worst invention ever developed for anyone who has to read a lot. Analysts unanimously abhor this method of printing.

COUNT IT OUT

While you're going over that script page by page and giving it the final once-over, also check the page count. Sometimes copy machines skip a page or two. No one notices until the reader realizes that the story doesn't follow from one page to the next. If the missing page includes crucial action or some information that's important to the set-up, the loss is critical. Even if no essential plot information is omitted, the reader will view a missing page as suggestive of a casualness on the part of the writer.

WHITE SPACE

After you've finished checking all this minutia, just when you're beginning to wonder if writing's about creativity or about clerical chores, flip through the script one more time. As you do this, do you see a lot of white space, or are the pages covered with descriptive copy? There should be lots of white space. The script pages shouldn't look crowded or cluttered. There is an apocryphal story that circulates around Hollywood. It is said that a well-known executive reads only dialogue. The story may not be true, but it's certain that many readers and executives skim as much material as they can. If most of your story's told in lengthy description, very little of it may be read. It's a good idea to maintain a positive ratio of white space to printed matter.

NUMBERING SCENES

There is a standard argument that arises whenever struggling writers convene. Some will insist scenes should be numbered. Others are equally convinced that scenes need no numbering. Additionally, there's disagreement about whether the scene numbers should be noted at both the right and left margins. These disputes can be easily resolved. Scene numbers are unnecessary.

Feature film scripts are written in master-scene format. The author begins each scene with the appropriate notation of the interior or exterior, time of day, and place. The scene is described, and the dialogue and action follow. These master scenes aren't numbered at all.

Television sitcom scripts note each act and scene with a number or a letter. On the other hand, feature film scenes are numbered by the person preparing the shooting script after the material has been purchased and is being prepared for production. Scene numbers are not needed prior to that.

To Be Continued

The use of the word "continued" at the bottom and top of every page isn't necessary and is becoming very uncommon. Again, this notation is added when the film's put into production, in order to aid camera direction, i.e., it lets the director of photography and the camera operator know whether to keep the camera rolling or maintain the same set-up although the end of a page of script has been reached.

Shots

Sometimes, in the opening pages of a script, detailed instructions for different camera shots are included. As the script progresses, however, fewer and fewer appear. This usually happens because the writer begins by picturing specifically how a scene should be shot, but as he gets into the story, the vision of each scene become less precise. The writer doesn't need to include any specific camera angles or particular shots, except of the most basic nature. You'll want only to distinguish when a shot should be long, medium, or close-up. Occasionally, the narrative demands a particular shot, such as a tracking or a POV.

Professional writers usually include "ANOTHER ANGLE" to break up dialogue or descriptive paragraphs. The director and the director of photography will decide what specific shots should be made. That's their expertise.

Asides

There is just one final note in this mechanical section. Now and then, immature scriptwriters regard their writing task as an informal, casual, odious exercise that must be gotten through in order for a fabulous screen story to be told. They let themselves get chummy with the reader by making little asides to them. For example, one writer offered the following:

> The car's gearshift suddenly slipped into neutral, and it began a slow descent down the hill. We knew this was coming, didn't we?

When an actor talks to the audience directly, it's called an "aside." He has suddenly stepped out of the world on stage, a world the audience is looking at through the "fourth wall," and reminded the theatergoers that they are watching a play. A writer does much the same thing when, in the midst of creating a story, he suddenly comments directly to the reader. This particular technique isn't endearing or professional.

Don't you feel better now? You've finished this chapter full of script mechanics, and it's hoped you've resolved a few problems yours may have had. Now, let's get on to more important script elements.

THE INTERMEDIATE

7

"You call that purling? You dropped a stitch."

Once your script looks good and its appearance makes a favorable impression on everyone who sets eyes on it, you face a tougher job. When a reader picks up a professional-looking script and starts reading, omissions and faults more complicated than appearance can land it in the "pass" file.

Keeping in mind that this book is not meant to be a writing manual—there are no secrets you can learn that will *guarantee* writing success—there are some common conventions and basic storytelling elements that you should be aware of, and generally conform to, if you want your work to be taken seriously by the people in the film industry who will be reading it.

GETTING LITERATE ABOUT IT

Back in the fifteenth century, Erasmus said, "God does not much mind bad grammar, but He does not take any particular pleasure in it."

This attitude toward grammar—and punctuation and usage—holds pretty true for today's Hollywood. Because a script is the working plan upon which a movie—a visual presentation—is built, scripts generally aren't required to maintain the same literary standards that are required of material whose final form will be in the print medium. Nonetheless, you should consider your screenplay as a semifinal form.

Since it has to be read before it can be put on celluloid, analysts needs to navigate your prose with ease. When a reader's tossed through a storm of multiple misspellings, awkward usage, and errors of grammar, "script sickness" grows with each turn of the page.

A reader at Warner Bros. recalled, "I've read lots of scripts with an error or two and a few typos. I don't mind them. But only once in all my eight years of reading did I, even tentatively, recommend a script that was essentially illiterate. I *didn't* recommend the writer, who seemed genuinely oblivious to the common rules of grammar; however, the script's premise seemed promising, so I recommended it as a story idea. Maybe the executives were just as irritated as I was with the writer's sloppy handling of the English language—they passed on the project."

Every analyst reacts differently to errors in this area. Some are tolerant, some not. Each has her particular likes and dislikes. Probably the wisest approach is to strive to make your script flawless. It still won't be perfect; that there will be a missed typo or spelling error somewhere in its one-hundred-plus pages is practically guaranteed. *You* may not be bothered when you violate the less/fewer rule, or the use of apostrophes, or the then/than distinction, but you don't know who may be reading your script, and whoever it is may just be a fanatic about the very rule you've disregarded.

If you're feeling a little unsure of yourself, begin your scriptwriting career by buying yourself an invaluable gift: a copy of Strunk and White's *Elements of Style*. Read it through three times—it's only eighty-five pages long. You may be more devoted to the visual than the written, but don't sell those building plans short and hope that analysts will read your mind and understand what you mean to say, even if you haven't said it. If someone can't read your blueprint, your project will never get constructed.

KEEP IT MOVING

CAMERA DESCRIPTIONS

Anyone who picks up your script should be able to read it and mentally watch it on screen. This means the reader should "see" the flow of the story without being bogged down by excessive material meant to be used by editors, cinematographers, and directors. Write a story script, not a shooting script. An assistant director or a unit production manager will work out the shooting specifics with the director and director of photography. For instance, an analyst may see the following:

> The camera tracks on the carpet, then angles up through the glass table and stops on Mazie's ample cleavage, then tracks through the glass! Goes over her shoulder, does a 180 turn, and we see a knife sticking out of Mazie's back through her $500 dress. On a Steadicam, the camera tracks down the back of the couch following the dripping blood. NEW ANGLE: from the kitchen to the living room, a shot of a fly on the kitchen ceiling. POV as the fly takes off and lands on the knife!

Excessive shot descriptions such as the one above aren't necessary, and they slow down the story's flow. More importantly, the director will consider the writer presumptuous for trying to usurp the creative challenges of his job. Contrast the above with this scene from *Chinatown:*

> On Gittes' desk, there are empty coffee cups, the summons and complaint—and the newspaper Gittes had brought with him from the barber shop.

The cinematographer is free of unnecessary shooting instructions and will create camera angles appropriate for the meaning of the shot to be conveyed.

Technically Speaking

There might be occasions when you need to describe technical information important to the plot. You may know everything possible about your arcane science, machine, or topic, but usually, the audience doesn't need to understand everything about it. Neither does the analyst.

Keep your prose nontechnical, brief, and essential to what will be seen and used on screen. For example, maybe you need to use a piece of obscure English law or a whatsit machine that performs some rare medical test; the law or the machine is important to your plot. If you feel you can't or shouldn't translate the law's meaning or the machine's function into everyday speech, are you sure you aren't showing off? Which is more important to you, to show off your knowledge, or to sell your script? Test out your rewrites on friends willing to indulge you. See if they understand what you're trying to explain.

THE SEEABLE

To keep the flow going, limit your descriptions to what's *seeable* on screen. When introducing or developing characters, forget about describing what they are thinking. How will we know this when we see them on screen? We won't. Show us. It's a movie, after all.

Ask yourself three times if the character's position on a particular topic is significant to the structure of the plot and if it is consistent with his or her personality. You may be just looking for an outlet for your own opinions about the said topic, however, expressing those feelings might not fit this story or these characters. After some candid soul searching, if you decide that your hero's position is important because it will play an important role in the story's development, then include a scene to make those feelings known, or write one of those seemingly innocuous reaction shots that tip the audience off to a character's opinions. You get the idea. By *dramatizing* your character's feelings, the reader or viewer will know right away how your character feels about a particular subject.

Always let your characters' actions and dialogue show us what kinds of people they are. Do they kick the cat when they enter the scene? That's a lot more revealing than to be told the same thing via the description.

This rule holds true with the mise en scene (the entire contents of each scene). Don't write that the weather's always been rainy in whatever locale you've placed your story if the rain is never seen. Don't even include the notation that it's raining outside. Unless that rain will have an effect on the story or the scene—we'll see it or hear it for some reason—don't mention it. If that rain doesn't work into the plot in some way or add a dimension to the characters' emotional states or to the story's theme, why include it? There is no reason. But if you decide rain is an absolute necessity, you needn't load down the "stage" directions with extensive descriptions. Just include it as part of setting each scene, e.g., ". . . the rain continues" or "rain hits the window panes loudly." To repeat, if you can't shoot it, don't write it.

DESIGNER CLOTHES AND SUVS

Excessive descriptions of appearance and clothing also put the brakes on the forward movement of your story. It's easier on the writer and the reader if you state right away what status or politics a character's dress and accessories reflect. Don't become a Neiman Marcus catalog copywriter in the middle of the suspense tale you're hoping will grip the reader.

Excessive and precise descriptions (unless they figure into the plot or the character in a *crucial* way) tell us more about the writer's ideas of wealth and glamour than they do about the character. Writing that a character "drives up in a late-model, expensive car" is plenty informative. The reader will get it. The exception to this rule is the handling of stereotypes. When and if you have stereotypical characters purposely included in your story, sometimes a particular type of car is a part of that stereotype. Then you want to include the car's make. Say, for example, your script includes a Hell's Angel type. You would probably want to include that he drives a Harley-Davidson.

By now, you might be completely intimidated about writing descriptions. Let's get more positive. Remembering that brevity is the spice of a screenplay's life, don't be afraid to write creative descriptions. You don't want to be so uniformly literal in your writing that there is no pleasure in reading it. Think, for instance, of the scene in *Chinatown* where Gittes leaves the bed he and Mrs. Mulray have just shared. He goes out and knocks out one of the taillights on her car. We don't quite know what he's up to until later, when she leaves and he follows her through the darkened streets of the city. The broken taillight acts like a beacon for him. The script description is simple, but Gittes' method of making Mulray's car easy to pursue is creative and makes this sequence more interesting than if Robert Towne had described the scene in detail, but omitted having Gittes break a taillight.

MONTAGES

Short, jump-cut, rapid scenes, usually written without dialogue, are trickier than they appear. On the one hand, they seem like an easy way to show a relationship developing or the preparatory steps for an upcoming action scene, but too often, they're a crutch for writers who want to cover some dull material quickly. Remember that the reader wants to get through montages even faster. They rarely contain essential story material that will tie into the plot or relationships later on.

One scene with carefully thought-out action can serve just as well as a montage to reveal a growing relationship or a set-up for subsequent action. For example, in *A Fish Called Wanda*, the writers could have used a montage of the robbers getting ready for their heist. Instead, there was a scene at the kitchen table during which the boss reviews three items in their plan. Kevin Kline's character, who is trying to sell himself as a slick operator, but who is actually a numskull, twice asks the boss to repeat an item. The sequence is much funnier and fresher, using this one scene, than it would have been dashing through a montage of tired sight gags showing the gang gathering their equipment, checking the guns, finding the hideout for the money, etc. Avoid montages most of the time.

FLASHBACKS AND DREAM SEQUENCES

Flashbacks, like montages, are often a crutch for a writer hoping to fill in a character's background that usually isn't really necessary to the story.

Too often, new writers who use flashbacks open their scripts with a brief scene set in the present and then flash back to an earlier time period. Sometimes, the script ends without returning to the present. More often, they switch back to the present, but the past action—most of the story—hasn't influenced or changed the present. Why have a flashback? It's better to simply open the script as a story set in the recent past or to be candid about the historical setting of the story.

When flashbacks are used, it's best if they're brief and form their own mini-subplot. Before including them, ask yourself, What purpose is the flashback serving? Is there another way—preferably through action— the same information can be conveyed? Flashbacks can destroy a story's momentum, especially when they distract from the story's primary tale.

In some films, like *War of the Roses*, the flashbacks *are* the plot, and they have a *significant* influence on the characters' present-day lives and circumstances at story's end. In other films, like *Fried Green Tomatoes*, two stories, one set in the past and the other contemporary, were combined. Even this unusual approach wasn't entirely satisfactory. The present-day story was shortchanged in many ways. More recently, films such as *Pleasantville* use a kind of time travel—in this one it's via the television—but essentially, it's a flashback. Other fantasy films like *The Matrix* and *Groundhog's Day* manipulate time by stopping, replaying, and rewinding events. These, too, are another form of flashback, or flashforward.

At least since the first season of *The X Files*, blurring the lines between reality, dreams, visions, electronic recreations, and paranormal experiences have taken over where the brain probes, sensory deprivation, hypnosis, and dream sequences of old left off. The purpose of many of these sequences is to fool the audience into believing the dramatized events are real. Before relying on these sequences, think through the decision carefully. Regardless of their ability to fool the audience or their shock value, these sequences, like flashbacks, generally keep your story movement in neutral. Also, since they've been the rage for the last few years, they may be on the way out of favor. If you do employ these techniques, make certain the analyst can follow your path, i.e., know in which state the characters reside at any given moment in the story, and don't let these excursions to Never Never (or Never Was) Land stop the forward flow of your story.

VOICE-OVERS AND NARRATION

Narration, so popular in the old film noirs, is always an iffy approach, though it's occasionally done, as it was in *High Fidelity*. Occasionally, there's a little narration used at the beginning of a film, as occurred in *Stand By Me*, but the focus quickly moves to the action. Generally, they aren't really necessary, and like dream sequences and flashbacks, they can become a crutch. If you're substituting words when you could use action, you're writing radio, not film. Whenever narration is included, it absolutely must serve a function in the story, and even then, any extended use of the narrator is hard to justify. Remember, too, there are people in the business that just flat hate narration.

SUMMING UP

George Bernard Shaw once said, "In literature, the ambition of the novice is to acquire the literary language; the struggle of the adept is to get rid of it." And in today's world, if literary pretense is diminishing—because no one's reading the classics anymore—it's being replaced by a hybrid, awkward form of language. Apparently, too many writers are watching too much television, specifically things like *Cops*. They've let terms like "perp" and "proceeded" replace the terms "the guy, man, and woman" and "walked, ran, and strode" that should have been used. It's no wonder that corkscrew usage shows up. We're assaulted with it every day. If it isn't coming from the television and advertising, it's coming from the bureaucrats we have to deal with or the commentators and "scholars" who constantly explain our own society to us in psychobabble or in the language of business and the legal field. Think of yourself as Shaw's adept and clear all this clutter out of your writing.

Beginning scriptwriters nearly always overwrite; there is too much description and too much dialogue. After you've wrestled through your epic and trimmed all the elements just discussed, see where else you can cut. Be merciless with your prose.

MAKING THE SCENES

LENGTH

Currently, the scenes in screenplays run about two to three pages. The old conventional eight- or ten-pager is probably too large a narrative chunk to tackle all at once. If your scenes run five or six pages, maybe you're trying to do too many things simultaneously. This is easy to solve. Clearly identify the purposes of the scene. Once you know what you're trying to achieve, break the long scene into two or three shorter ones, each of which serves fewer plot functions.

Strive, too, for brevity in dialogue. As one development executive said, "Write as little as possible." Long speeches are unnatural; most people don't speak that way. Two or three lines are more natural and realistic. But in those rare instances when the story must include a long speech, break it up visually on the page. When speakers talk, there is always something going on in the audience—you need only go to church on Sunday to learn that. By inserting simple stage or camera directions, or by including brief reaction shots, the speech will appear less intimidating, and the script won't devolve into a talking heads syndrome. For example:

```
                    TERRORIST
          . . . and so my fellow terrorists,
          we must stand firm and insist on
          a pension plan! More perks! More
          training in explosives and safety.
          Regular hours, stock options in
          companies we don't blow up or
          take hostages from.


He stops, belches. The audience is oblivious;
they're talking in low tones to each other.


                    TERRORIST (con't)
          We've gotta get binding
          arbitration for our services and
          iron-clad contracts.
```

```
Two men in the audience start playing chess.
Others watch.

                TERRORIST (con't)
           We've put ourselves on the line
           once too often. We deserve
           more than we're getting! (BEAT)
           And what about vacations?

The crowd perks up at this.
```

To run the above dialogue in one long column will provoke dread in readers. When they spot it, they know they're in for an "author's lecture." And frankly, listening to lectures you didn't pay to hear is bad enough; reading one is practically impossible.

ACTION

If your script includes a big action scene, don't toss it away by writing something like, "Right here should be the biggest gang fight you ever saw" or "At this point, all the planes attack." You most assuredly don't want to wrap up an action scene in a sentence such as these if that scene is the story's climax. Writing an important action scene in this manner will diminish its impact, and it makes you sound as if you're uninformed or too lazy to think it through and figure out how to write it.

When guns are important to the scene, you should know one from another. You don't need to join the N.R.A., but you should be able to distinguish an AK47 from a .38. It's even better if you know which guns have what reputations.

To choreograph a commando attack or similar scene, work out the logistics in your mind, or on paper, before you write it. Then write it and rewrite it, paring and refining it.

Following the action of lots of different characters, in different locations, in a variety of vehicles, toting different makes of guns can drive a reader to distraction. If the reader can't get a picture of the battle and has to go back over the material to keep track of who's where and who's been killed or wounded, it's frustrating. Even though you know the director probably will change everything in the scene, including the location, you must describe the chaos you want to convey with clarity, coherence, and brevity.

If you have a complicated action scene to describe, say a gang of burglars is breaking into a top security government building, you need to describe how it's being done. Again, think it through. If the break-in isn't described in realistic terms, you'll lose the audience's good will and willingness to believe in the story. And if the description of the action scene runs on for several lines, break up the paragraph with either a simple double space or a camera direction such as "ANOTHER ANGLE."

RAZZLE DAZZLE

Remembering that your script will be read before it's put on screen, dazzling the readers along the way will improve your chances of selling the material. For that reason, try to include at least one scene (the more the better) that will sweep the readers off their collective feet with its cleverness, uniqueness, and dialogue.

In the words of the late Gary DeVore, writer of such films as *Mean Season*, *Running Scared*, and *Back Roads* and former head of production for DeLaurentiis Entertainment Group, "Every script should have one unforgettable scene and at least one line of unforgettable dialogue." Think of the scenes you remember from movies. Think of all the quotable movie lines you've heard.

If you can manage Herculean creativity for at least one scene, and produce a dazzler, it'll aid your script in many ways.

LOVE STORIES AND SEX SCENES

THE LOVE THEME

Nearly every script written has a love story in it. Sometimes it's the central story, sometimes it exists for the convenience of the leading character, and sometimes it's included so a sex scene can be a part of the story. They're a challenge to write well.

Getting assigned to read a "romantic comedy" often brings moans from analysts, because they know most romantic comedies are neither funny enough or romantic enough to sustain interest to the final page. Often, the romantic half of a romantic comedy resembles nothing a reader has ever experienced personally or secondhand via conversations with friends.

To write a convincing love story that will speak to your audience with conviction, the writer should have actually experienced romance. No, not the high school crush kind of romance, not the short term, noncommittal college kid kind, but the grown-up people kind. The *English Patient* or *Notting Hill* kind. The kind that reveals that the writer understands and appreciates, or at least tolerates, how the sexes work, individually and jointly. Remember screenwriters Garson Kanin and Ruth Gordon? They had a long, successful love affair and wrote classic romantic comedies.

THE GENERIC LOVE OBJECT

Many times, the most disappointing element of a script is the love story. There is such a sameness to so many of them, you would think the writers, inevitably male, all consulted the same muse. These scripts go something like this: In the opening pages of the story, the hero is confronted with the problem that fuels the plot. In the midst of this, he sees 1) the most beautiful woman in the world. She has 2) a perfect shape, 3) perfect clothes. She is usually 4) wealthy, 5) drives a new car, 6) is willing, nay anxious, to scramble her brains out between the sheets, and 7) she's better at it than any other woman in the universe. Occasionally, she's feisty, but usually she pretty much disappears until the plot calls for another appearance, or the hero needs a bit of loving to make himself feel better about the mess he's trying to resolve. She rarely helps solve the problem, but she offers comfort; she sometimes has to be saved, but not always; and she loves the man, although she occasionally leaves or double-crosses him.

The men who create this Stepford femme fatale seem unable to translate to the page the real women they know. (And readers often suspect the writer hasn't had a date since his mother insisted he take the neighbor girl to his grade school graduation party.) Nor does it appear that the writers have the slightest understanding of flesh and blood women. The rest of the script may be as realistic as the nightly news, but the love interest is an objectified and idealized view of the fair sex. Sometimes it's even worse. Sometimes the love story is downright laughable, and the reader can only conclude that the writer's emotional development is permanently jammed at about age fourteen. This presentation of the feminine love interest equals those trusty, manly men that romp through the pages of the most formulaic and adolescent of romance novels.

JUST SKIP IT

If you've never been in love; if you've never had a relationship that lasted more than two months; if you've never met someone who made your heart do loop-de-loops and with whom you had a madcap, passionate weekend during which neither of you wore any clothes, you might consider relegating your love stories to sub-subplot status.

You can still turn out great scripts without pasting on some unbelievably stilted romance. There are lots of good movies in which the love story was very sweet and adolescent. Remember *Star Wars?* And there are films like *A Few Good Men* that only hint at love. Lots of terrific movies have no love story at all, like *Pi* and *Men with Guns*. Some films revolve around a use-me, use-you sex story like, *The Grifters* or *Wild Thing*. As you already know, it's damn difficult to write about something you know nothing about. The reader will recognize material that seems inspired more by romantic fantasies than by real life.

RAISING THE TEMPERATURE

Sex scenes offer another challenge. Obviously, they aren't the easiest things to write or to film. If you include a sex scene in your script, it's probably to show 1) a couple falling in love, 2) a couple profoundly in love, or 3) an erotic mood or coupling. Because it's too easy to get a response you hadn't intended, you have to proceed gingerly, so your reader or audience will get the intended message.

If readers laugh when their temperatures are supposed to be rising, or if they get uncomfortable when they're supposed to be cheering on the budding love affair you're writing about, you're in trouble. If you haven't had a variety of sexual experiences (watching porn on the Net or on TV doesn't count, and neither does reading *Playboy*), you will probably be better off keeping your sex scenes pretty conventional. On the other hand, even if you've had a variety of sexual experiences, you're better off keeping your sex scenes conventional. The sex you depict shouldn't be offensive. You're writing for a mass audience.

Finally, please, keep your sexual hang-ups and weird practices out of the script—save them for your personal, private pleasure.

THE REALITY MEDIUM

ENHANCING REALITY

Cinema is called the realistic medium, but we all know this isn't entirely true. We accept that movies take liberties with reality. Think of the last screen fistfight you saw. The hero, after taking a beating that would put any real person in traction for life, gets up, fights back effortlessly, and vanquishes his attackers. We know this fight isn't realistic, and many people decry this kind of fantasy for serving mankind badly. Similar, but louder, concerns are expressed about screen gun battles. This expansion of reality is one of those conventions that is so much a part of film, it's routinely included in movies and accepted as valid storytelling.

Since heroes are usually required to be somewhat larger than life, writers are permitted to color outside the lines of reality to tell their story. The degree to which a hero's abilities are enhanced depends on the script. In a live-action cartoon, such as *The Fifth Element*, the sky's not even the limit. But if your story is set in the more realistic confines of everyday life, as it was in the films *The Insider* or *My Best Friend's Wedding*, your hero's physical actions must be much truer to the capabilities of ordinary men.

The important thing to remember is the sense of appropriateness. If a story that is written fairly close to real-life proportions suddenly includes a scene that's straight out of *Superman*, it will throw off the tone completely and become a jarring interruption for the reader or viewer. This happened in *Lethal Weapon II*.

The first *Lethal Weapon* enhanced reality; the second accidentally became more cartoon-like. Although the *Lethal Weapon II* characters couldn't disobey the physical laws that prevail in the world, suddenly at the film's climax, Mel Gibson's character pulls down a cliff house with a rope and a pickup truck. Looking at the steel-beamed support, imbedded in solid rock below, you can only titter and realize the movie has unwittingly become a cartoon.

EMBROIDERING ON REALITY

It's also acceptable to take liberties with the tools, techniques, and paraphernalia of various professions. For example, during your research, a technician tells you that certain kinds of data are unavailable on a computer screen. But for your story to advance in a visually interesting way, or because it seems the most efficient way to convey some vital information quickly, you might want that information to appear on a computer screen. So you show it on the screen. You've expanded reality. You haven't created an impossibility, you've just embroidered on accepted technology.

ELEMENTARY PHYSICS

Don't forget the basic laws of physics. An otherwise well-written script included a scene in which two goons wanted to shut down the power to a building in a Western city. The script describes them as being in the desert. They cut through a power pole, wrap some rope around the wires, attach the rope to their bumper, and drive off, felling the pole and breaking the wires. This act was supposedly committed by henchmen for a powerful, influential group. What's more, the men in the building to which the power was cut immediately jumped in their cars and drove to the desert power lines to find the source of their trouble.

There are so many things wrong with this scene that it should be part of a Three Stooges movie. Think about it. Physically, as in physics, this wire-downing ploy wouldn't work. Quickly, here's some of the reasons why: 1) How do the guys in the building whose power is cut know exactly where to go to find the culprits? 2) How do the goons know which way the current is running? 3) Main lines in the desert generally feed maybe half a city or more. 4) These wires aren't the size of that extension cord you keep in the bottom drawer in the kitchen—they're heavy and thick; their weight helps stabilize the poles, and breaking them by pulling on them will take incredible thrust. 5) There's more than a good chance the weight and strength of the wires will force the back end of the car—that is if the wires are attached to something more solid then a bumper—off the ground. And 6) most assuredly, these idiots will get electrocuted.

If you flunked high school physics, you really ought to do a little basic research before you write about complicated maneuvers. Once you know what's physically possible, you can then stretch the scene to movie proportions.

SCIENCE FICTION

Science fiction presents special problems. Too often, authors of scripts that tell an out-of-this-world tale haven't got their physics in order. This might seem too elementary to even warrant discussion, but in one unfortunately memorable script, outerspace aliens came to earth possessing superhuman powers. It soon became apparent that whatever narrative problems the writer came upon he solved by having the aliens possess a power to solve them. It wasn't a good script; it was lazy writing.

When you create a new world, you have to work out what physical laws your beings or your worlds are going to obey. Even Superman is consistent. He can do almost anything, but he always stops to change into costume, and he's vulnerable to kryptonite. Batman, Spiderman, Spawn, Betelgeuse. They all have limitations.

IDEAL SOCIETIES

A variation of this principle needs to be honored when you create stories about earth-bound colonies or new societies established away from ordinary society as we know it. In one script, a writer depicted the creation of a new society getting established on an island. He lost the reader when he included materials that would be impossible for the inhabitants to possess. It worked for *Gilligan's Island* because that was supposed to be silly, but if you have some notions about the ideal society and you write a script dramatizing its creation, you have to restrict yourself to what's available to your characters in their locale and chronological setting.

For instance, if your story's going to take place on a South Seas island, don't have your characters chopping down fir trees for their Christmas celebration. There are no fir trees in the South Seas. Now, if you have one of your characters secret away a potted fir sapling that he tries to grow on the island in anticipation of the annual holiday, that's something else. That becomes a subplot or a running gag.

This same caution applies to stories of people stranded or abandoned in some area remote from civilization, 7-Eleven stores, and cellular phones.

DOWN-TO-EARTH REALISM

Failing to do simple research is a much more common problem in regular scripts than it is in science fiction or idealistic society stories. The writer resorts to stereotypes or blatantly misrepresents characters or places because he hasn't gotten away from his PC long enough to actually explore his topic.

One script told the story, supposedly based on an actual event, of a contemporary southwestern Indian man accused of murder. The writer apparently had never been around contemporary American Indians. He wrote that they killed animals only when they needed food. As anyone who lives in the Southwest can tell you, contemporary American Indians get most of their food from supermarkets. A little later in the story, the heroine explains that "Indians only burn dead wood." Forgetting for the moment that green wood doesn't burn well no matter who lights the match, a little dab of research, just a little, and the writer would have learned how dated, mindlessly idealistic, and flat wrong he was. In Arizona alone, one Native American tribe owned a huge logging company. No, they didn't burn dead wood, they cut down trees and sold them for a profit—like regular businessmen. Throughout the script, the writer revealed such an ignorance of his topic that he unknowingly became an embarrassment and insulted American Indians in general.

Some solid research will do wonders to enhance the believability of your story, and the reader will be pleased that he gets a "free" lesson in physics, technology, history, or whatever. But if it sounds like you don't know what you're talking about, your solid credibility will move directly to a gaseous state and disappear.

OTHER TOPICS

HEAD BANGERS

Each day as you interact with your fellow man, it may appear that he's pretty dumb, and you may have read studies that the average SAT score has fallen to dangerous depths. Keep in mind that even those who lack sheepskins and whose I.Q.s are in single digits catch on pretty quickly to characters' emotions and the plot turns in a movie. You don't need to hit them over the head with your ideas, characters, or plot twists. A recently-submitted script reassured the reader every few pages that the hero's mission was dangerous. Enough already! One description, two tops, is sufficient. Neither the reader or the viewer will forget.

Another script came in about Mexican-Americans. By page 30, the author had repeated a dozen times that these people were of a higher moral order and could do no wrong. The author needed only to tell us this information once—preferably through the actions of the hero. The other reminders are simply redundant (and embarrassing, since any Mexican-American who read it probably would be outraged at the primitive portrayal of their people and impatient with the script's falseness, since every ethnic group has its share of noble, despicable, ordinary, and extraordinary people). You've heard the old saw, about never overestimating the intelligence of the audience. Better that you don't underestimate it. No one, readers and moviegoers alike, appreciates being talked down to.

EXPOSING THE BLUEPRINT

Authors have to inform the audience of particular pieces of information. It's called exposition, or less formally, laying pipe. Most exposition, like back stories or the set-up, is handled in dialogue and action. Sometimes, however, there is additional information that needs to be conveyed. It ranges from the simple definition of an obtuse term to explaining how a machine or a character "works." If this, or any, exposition is poorly handled, red flags pop up all over the page screaming "exposition!" An example is the movie, *Blue Chips*. Nick Nolte's character told us more than we needed to know about the situation and didn't show us enough. In *Class Action*, the brilliant thirty-four-year-old lawyer, who's about to be made a partner, asks another character, "What's a bean counter?" Excuse me? Everyone in the audience knows. How did that bit of contemporary cultural slang bypass a well-informed character? If the author felt the audience wouldn't know what a bean counter was, there are plenty of other ways to handle defining it rather than in this obvious manner.

To set up the plot, the author may need to explain how a machine works. Stay away from characters giving long-winded explanations. If you do, the exposition flag will fly, and every analyst will have to guzzle lattes to stay awake. There are at least a couple of ways to avoid raising the flag. One way is to have the machine go on the blink.

                       BOSS
What's wrong?

                     WORKER
The autoergotron won't work.

                       BOSS
Why not?

                     WORKER
It's not transforming straw
into gold.

                       BOSS
Well damn it, if it's not working,
then call the repair dwarf. Now!

Another approach is to have two characters argue about the usefulness, value, or ethical problems of a machine. In their shouting, they can explain just what it is that the damn thing does.

Delineating the author's message is a more common exposition problem than either of the above. This thesis is usually the reason the author wrote the script. You know these scenes, they come at about twenty-three minutes into every television sitcom. The characters realize Something Important About Life. The "author's message" flag waves like crazy. In a screenplay, you must be more subtle. Your message, the script's theme, must be woven throughout the action, and if you've told your story well, the audience will have gotten it by the denouement.

FAD CATCHERS

Attempting to write to a trend or in anticipation of one is a bad idea. You've got to figure it like this: With incredible luck (emphasis on incredible), the time it takes to get a film produced is about three years. So, if you've written a trendy piece, chances are the trend will be spent by the time your story reaches the big screen. We've all heard at least one story of a top writer who took ten years to get his favorite project to the big screen. As a beginner, you can count yourself lucky if you get any film made in five years. So, you'd probably be wise to treat trends as if they were a bad case of hypoglycemia. Remember that once-trendy affliction?

Only once in a blue moon does a trend survive for a couple of years or get revived. One incident will serve to illustrate the point. In 1986, at DeLaurentiis, *Tougher Than Leather—Run DMC* was submitted. The reader hated the script for a variety of reasons. More importantly, the reader felt that since rap music had passed into the thirty-second-commercial arena, it was no longer cutting-edge material. There would be no audience for the musically-based film. The studio passed on the script. But rap music revived in 1988. Could a rap-music movie again be viable? Was the blue moon rising? It seemed so. In its revival, however, rap was different. Its new interpretation was much more mainstream and light-hearted. *Tougher Than Leather* was made by another studio that assumed there was still a rap audience out there. True to form, though, the movie never did any real business and sank without a box office ripple.

The folly of writing to or anticipating trends is most obvious in two lambada movies released in 1990. During the six months before the movies were made, the popular media kept broadcasting pieces about this hot new dance craze. Sure enough, two movies were quickly thrown together. But this fad dance never took off among the general public, and so the movies, which anticipated that it would, had no audience. It seemed that the trend declined, even among the aficionados, before the flicks were finished.

MONEY, MONEY, MONEY

Anticipating the budget necessary for your film is an exercise in futility. No one ever sold a script based solely on the cost to produce it. Concentrate on writing a good story; let the studio worry about the budget. The cost of a movie isn't your responsibility, marketing your gem is. If you've written a huge space epic, don't submit it to a company that makes only ten-million-dollar movies. Write the story you want to tell without regard to budget. Then, when you're ready to sell it, find an appropriate studio.

THE TITLE WILL TELL

Sometimes you change the title of your screenplay repeatedly; sometimes the title comes as pure inspiration. You might want to try out your title on a few friends before you chisel it in stone. Don't underestimate its importance. As Kim Ohanneson said, "A distinctive title is unforgettable." The title ought to be appropriate for the genre of film you're writing. By trying out the title on your friends, you'll find out if it implies a tone to your movie that you didn't intend. For example, sometimes a script title can read like a comedy, but the story is anything but funny. Other titles sound downright tragic, but the story's as lightweight as a cream puff with no filling. Think for a minute of the difference between *Jaws* and *A Fish Called Wanda*. Even if you were one of the ten people in the world who didn't see either of these films, you can figure out from the titles which one is the comedy. How about *The Money Tree, It Grows on Trees, Greed,* or *Wall Street*? All these films are about money, but there's not much doubt which films are comedies and which aren't.

For good or ill, many film titles tend to be short, so they quickly convey the movie's high concept: *Mission to Mars, Gossip, 28 Days.* Sometimes titles are familiar phrases or clichés that have an ordinary meaning and also reflect the theme of the story or refer to an additional, sometimes a symbolic, meaning: *Keeping the Faith, Rules of Engagement, The Devil's Advocate.* Of course, the real winner in the title sweepstakes is an original turn of phrase, like *Back to the Future* or *Sex, Lies and Video Tape*, that moves right into the language and into the copy of half the world's journalists.

THE HEART OF IT

Finally, you should, so they say, write from the heart. What does that mean, exactly? Mostly, the notion of writing from the heart is an erstwhile romantic sentiment and a warning to the novice. If you're a professional writer, accustomed to making a living by putting words on paper, your heart doesn't necessarily have to be present and accounted for when you write.

There's a story told about Laurence Olivier, considered by some to be the greatest twentieth-century actor, when he was working on *Marathon Man* with Dustin Hoffman. Hoffman was completely involved in preparing for a scene, getting inside the character, tiring himself out so he would have an appropriately haggard look. Olivier, opposed to such elaborate tactics, walked by, saw him, and said: "Don't live it, just do it."

If you're a novice, however, writing about that which you care deeply is important. Otherwise, you won't have the will to continue the campaign to sell it. Completing over a hundred pages of narrative is a battle, especially for those with no practice at it. There is no guarantee that just because you really care, the script will be good or will succeed, but you're more likely to fight for it when called on to do so.

There's a second advantage to writing from the heart. When you write about something you care nothing about, it's usually apparent to those who read it. Your work gets immediately discounted in the mind of the reader. But if you love something, your writing will reflect your passion.

Most important, if you write with passion, there's a real chance you can move the reader. If you can engage the analyst's mind and emotions, you've hooked 'em!

THE COMPLICATED

8

"I want this whole ridiculous story told by one person.
Is there anybody here who thinks they can handle it?"

Meticulously following conventional formatting and polishing the incidental elements will get you two-thirds there. But like a car with a great paint job and optional extras, it still needs a finely-tuned engine and high-grade gasoline to make it fire on all cylinders.

When asked what they felt was the most common script problem they encountered, the answers from analysts, writers, and producers varied. A reader at a major studio found that many scripts had "an uninteresting start and no way of getting to act three." For Ted Dodd, "writing screenplays about characters we don't care about" was a common shortcoming. Scripts that are yet one more version of the current box office winner is another problem he finds more often than he cares to. Chris Meindl agrees that "people write mostly derivations of other things," although he feels that the Hollywood system "is hardly geared to reward originality." Frank Balkin adds that too many scripts he reads fail to make "every character, every scene, every line of dialogue *crucial*." Several other problems were mentioned, but the majority of analysts agreed with the above comments.

Most studios and production companies have a scale that analysts use to rate the premise, story line, structure, character, and dialogue. These are the areas that must be fine-tuned so your vehicle will roar down the straightaway to fame and fortune.

PREMISES

When someone says, "What if . . . ," the idea for a story has sprung to life somewhere in the imagination. What if the post office was secretly. . . . What if the doctor down the street was really. . . . What if in the luggage compartment of planes. . . . What if a young opera singer's voice was suddenly. . . . You get the idea.

Stories start in other ways also. Maybe you have heard someone say, "You wouldn't believe my grandfather's life in Alaska." "All that Jamie went through with the hurricane and the fires and the floods could fill a book." "How did Aunt Mary manage to get out of Germany in 1935?" "Remember what a scandal it was when the mayor and that woman he promoted. . . ." "Tommy was so in love with that girl who jilted him, he. . . ." Stories are sparked by such comments and can form the premise of the script that you'll eventually write.

In the scoring box on coverage forms, the word "premise" is listed, but in conversations and pitch meetings, it's often referred to as the concept. Think of the premise or the concept as the foundation upon which you build a story.

You probably have also heard of "high concept" movies. This term is used when the premise that drives the story is easy to grasp (a one-sentence, or shorter, summary lets you know exactly what kind of film it is), it is highly commercial, and usually pretty expensive. *Matrix*, *Rules of Engagement*, and *EDtv* are all high concept pictures. This kind of film often earns big bucks for writers. Since many recent high concept films haven't done as well as expected at the box office (they have to pull in buckets of dough just to cover their expenses), some in the industry feel that the era of the action genre may be waning. The success of *American Beauty*, *Cider House Rules*, *All About My Mother*, *Clerks*, and others lends credence to those who believe there's been a shift, at least for now, away from a concentration of high concept films. The exception, of course, seems to be the summer movies, which always include three or four big action flicks.

More script analysts report that they had read more scripts powered by a terrific idea with little narrative support than competently written scripts with a weak idea. As Ohanneson said, "I definitely see great ideas buried in mediocre scripts." David Weinstein feels, "A great idea can't carry a poorly realized script." Most analysts said that although they don't usually recommend scripts that feature a solid idea poorly realized, they make note of the intriguing premise in their comments.

This isn't always the case. Randy Schmidt, an analyst with Largo Entertainment until that company disbanded, said that, "Largo specialized in action movies, so if a premise is good, everything else can be brought up to par by rewrites." He clarified that when a good premise comes wrapped in an inferior script, the "original writers are usually fired and new writers hired" to fix it.

As Ted Dodd, who's also produced films, said, "It's hard to sell a script that doesn't have an idea that stands out. The two-line pitch has to include the premise that will sell it. The chance of getting it sold without a good idea is slim at the studios."

So what do you do if you're short of "what if" scenarios and your family's as dull as wallpaper paste? What is a good idea, and how do you find one? Can you find one? Script ideas seem to happen spontaneously, anytime, anywhere. We all encounter events, places, people, and processes that spark ideas. Most of us let them slip through our minds and forget them as quickly as they occur; however, there are some things you can do to bolster this creative moment.

WRITE IT

When an idea occurs to you, write it down—even if it seems silly. Write it down, add any other thoughts you have about it, then set it aside. A week later, look at it again. If it still seems silly to you, throw it away. If it doesn't, keep it. If you get really fired up about an idea the moment it pops into your head, sit down immediately and write what comes to mind. Later on, if the idea isn't as wonderful as it seemed when you were writing it, you can throw it out. Nothing's been lost. Don't talk the idea dry. It will lose its interest and urgency if you talk about it excessively with friends or family.

CURIOUSER AND CURIOUSER

Be curious about everything you see. Ask yourself, "Why?" When you watch people, ask yourself questions about their behavior, make up stories to go along with their actions and faces, imagine what they might be doing, thinking, or feeling. When you read newspaper articles or watch television magazine shows, create different scenarios from the information given. Ask the questions the interviewer doesn't. Ask yourself what would have happened if one of the people featured in the story had done something differently.

THE ABCs OF READING

Nearly every script analyst that was surveyed for this book suggested that writers read—everything. More often, analysts and producers urged writers to read books. It broadens your field of knowledge, it offers new insight into events or experiences, it keeps you up-to-date about what's going on in the world, and it can be instructive in the use of language, description, character depiction, and dialogue. It can spark story ideas. Your reading should also include screenplays. Randy Schmidt feels that "one of the most valuable things you can do is read a lot of screenplays." The writer might find that "the ideas he thought were so great might be revealed as predictable, awful, and clichéd."

STOP, LOOK, AND LISTEN

Some people measure a good writer by how quiet they are, not how entertaining they can be. Writers need to observe life: how people behave, the way they speak, what's not spoken, what moves them to action, how individuals move physically, and all other overt human behavior. All these observations can lead to ideas for stories as well as improved characters, but you'll never hear or see them if you spend too much time doing the talking.

PLOWING THE BACKYARD

Instead of tormenting yourself trying to come up with a big-action film for Keanu Reeves or Brendan Fraser, (someone's probably already written and sold it anyway), look at your life and the things that happen to you, your friends, and your family. Remember *Clerks, Swingers,* and *High Fidelity?* Consider the things that could happen in this setting. There are ideas there, maybe even one Brendan would want to do.

LOOKING BEYOND THE BACKYARD

If you eschew the reality-based film and you're intent on writing big action or a thriller, find out what's already been done. Make a list of all the plots that have been used. Then, when you're putting your story together, strive for new combinations and types of characters, new twists and turns, and new realms and venues where murder and mayhem, crime and passion might erupt.

THINK DIVERGENTLY

Do exercises in divergent thinking. As an example, list all the uses of, say, a piece of paper. How many can you list? Push yourself to think of the improbable, the unconventional, the funny, serious, and oddball. Do the same exercise with an event you've experienced. Try coming up with all the possible conclusions that might transpire from the event. Think of all the possible responses the people you know might have to something that happens or something that is said to them. You might accidentally run across an idea for a story. You might not, but thinking of many possibilities clears a little more ground to cultivate for ideas.

WATCH THEM ALL

Many analysts and writers suggest that hopeful writers see lots of movies. You can learn about storytelling from them. You can see what's already been done to death. You can learn something about creating character and writing dialogue.

Once you've got an idea that strikes your fancy, assess it, then put it to a couple of tests. Script analysts automatically and unconsciously use these tests when they read scripts.

HANGING A STORY ON IT

Test #1. Will the premise carry a 120-page story? Or does the concept sputter to a dead stop by page 6 or 27 or 53 or 79? There may be no dramatic center to your idea. It simply may not be big enough for a full-length movie. You have to determine if it can be expanded. Is there a subplot that can be added to help prop up the main story? One reason many spec television pilot scripts fail is that the premises don't promise the possibility that dozens of stories can be spun off from them.

BELIEVE IT OR NOT

Test #2. As a reader at Warner Bros. said, too many scripts she reads are based on ideas that are "implausible and unbelievable." How do you know if your idea will pass the plausibility test? This is a hard one to answer, because Hollywood, in its quest for new twists, seems to be reaching the limit of believable premises.

Blink seems to have pushed the envelope, with its story of a blind woman whose sight is restored. She witnesses a murder, then experiences something called "after sight," which makes her unsure whether or not she's seen the actual murder. Since when does the cornea record images and later play them back like a videotape recorder? Later on, she doesn't know if the murderer's attacked her or if she imagined him attacking her. She never bothers to check for bruises and contusions. Why doesn't anyone question whether or not she's hallucinating? No one in the film, shot with low-level lighting, bothers to tell her that if you want to aid your sight, you put light on the object you want to see. Even people with 20/20 vision know that. Yet, the film, based on the blind/not blind premise, was made.

Then there's *Indecent Proposal*, which, as one screenwriter said, "had a terrible premise and no redeemable characters, yet succeeded, because the idea is so provocative to so many people." Why on earth would any over-the-hill millionaire pay one million dollars to sleep with a pretty woman when, no doubt, there are gobs of beautiful women—of all stripes and moralities—that would sleep with him for free, knowing who he is and that his bank balance could purchase a small country. It's ridiculous when you think about it for more than a split second. Maybe no one did. Without the heat of Robert Redford, Woody Harrelson, and Demi Moore, this film probably wouldn't have made it through the development process.

Some scripts with bad premises will always be developed in Hollywood, especially if the story is well-executed. *Indecent Proposal* is proof of that; so is *Hot Tubs II*. But your work shouldn't be among them. As a beginner, you will want to write as believably as possible without being dull. The script analyst has to buy the idea, and if it seems silly, outlandish, or fails to feature characters who behave within the limits of human behavior, you will have a tough time getting high marks.

One way to help you evaluate whether your idea is worth building a story around is to tell it to a friend or someone whose judgment you trust. Pitch them your two-line idea, and see how they respond. Don't just listen to their reaction; watch their face as they listen to you. If they aren't buying it, you may have an idea that's too absurd to be developed. As a director of development said, "Some writers don't seem to have asked themselves the question, 'Is my story worth telling?'" Make sure yours is.

STALE BREAD

More common than absurd premises are ideas that were threadbare before you were born. Readers and producers hate finding stories exhausted of their interest because of repeated interpretations of the premise.

Television's disease-of-the-week movies ran their course for longer then they deserved. Many analysts report reading too many scripts that are rehashes of whatever movie is currently making money at the box office. As a reader at one studio confessed, "With these scripts, you know how the screenplay will end before you get to page 5." On the other hand, being excessively original is not necessarily the road to commercial success in Hollywood. As a reader at an important company so aptly put it, "The joy of recognition is greater than the joy of surprise." The lesson here is to stay away from the trite *and* the bizarre.

PLOT AND STRUCTURE

If it's true that no story gets started without the spark of an idea, it's also true that it won't run the distance without a finely tuned plot that's structurally sound.

You want your story to fascinate readers, and later viewers, until the very end. To succeed at that, your story has to have a plot with enough complications and unexpected twists and turns to engage the reader until all the pieces are put in place in the final pages.

THE BASICS

We have all listened to good storytellers at one time or another. These people know how to tell a tale that captures our interest, leads us into the elements of the story, lays on unforeseen occurrences, then zooms in with the punch line.

Writing good scripts has a lot in common with good storytelling, only it is more formalized. Unlike stage plays, the curtain doesn't come down between acts at a movie theater, nonetheless, writing in acts is an accepted practice in Hollywood, adhered to more by some than others.

No less of an expert than Aristotle recommended in the *Poetics* that dramatic works should have "a beginning, middle, and an end." That is basically the three-act structure. A more colorful and clarifying explanation of the three-act structure was offered by producer Lawrence Turman: "Act one, get the hero in a tree. Act two, throw rocks at him. Act three, get him down."

Chris Meindl believes that for the purpose of breaking-in in Hollywood, writing scripts in three acts is necessary. "After you are established and you have mastered the form, then you can experiment." The director of development at a large production company feels that sticking with the three-act structure isn't always necessary, "but most commercial projects are written that way, and development executives and readers look for it." She goes on to say, "Writers should master the conventional structure first, then deviate."

Many analysts don't necessarily notice or want to notice the act breaks, but feel, as one reader does, that, "for lack of a better option," taking the three-act approach is the best. Another reader at one major studio agreed, but added that while he appreciated "writers trying to do otherwise, it's a hard sell" if a script doesn't follow the standard approach. Ted Dodd summed it up best when he said that while screenplays should follow the three-act structure, writers "don't have to be fanatics about it."

Those that dissent from the three act convention felt that the whole concept of acts ran counter to the way movies operate, but until you are a master of the craft, you are probably better off if you stick with the three-act approach as a way to organize your material into workable chunks.

The three-act structure provides an organizing device for your plot. You know that in act one, you must set up the story, the characters, and introduce the problem or conflict to be resolved or the goal to be met. In act two, characters are developed, complications arise as the hero tries to solve the problem or achieve his goal, and the tension rises, until it appears that all is lost. In act three, your hero must prevail, resolving the conflict or meeting his goal, and he must emerge from the miasma a changed person.

The progression of the story from beginning to end is often referred to as the story arc. The apex point of the arc is reached at the story's climax. Each event that turns the plot and moves it toward its conclusion is called a story beat or a plot point. Additionally, each scene has an arc, the apex of which is reached when the purpose of that scene is fulfilled.

The trick is making all this happen in an orderly manner. The best way to achieve a well-wrought story is, according to a reader, "outline, outline, outline. It's critical." For a senior vice president at a well-known production company, there are two things to consider when developing plot: "First, think before you write, and second, do a very detailed outline with scene breakdowns."

Neither of these development people felt that an outline would be restrictive. As the vice president said, "You don't have to be beholden to your outline, but a scene breakdown will show you where you have holes and pacing problems." As you write, your characters will sometimes say things you hadn't planned, and ideas for scenes that hadn't been outlined will occur. It's all right to go with your instinct, because your outline will prevent you from wandering away from your primary story.

When developing your plot, be cognizant of the following items. They can earn your script a fast ticket to the "pass" pile.

WE'VE SEEN THIS ALL BEFORE

Predictability is a real sleep inducer for those who read scripts. As one analyst put it, "The most common error writers make is developing predictable people relying on clichéd events." Scripts that opt for the obvious are sure to lose a reader's interest.

As an example, most of us talk things over with people at dinner or while we are around the house. In a screenplay, however, that is a pretty uninteresting approach. Get your characters out of the restaurant and into more interesting settings. Even better, get them into action. If you can substitute the dialogue with action, that's better yet. Write the scene without dialogue. See if it's possible. Filmmakers constantly strive for the unusual and fresh, because they know it holds our attention more readily. In your story, don't simply duplicate what ordinary people do, take it a notch farther up the scale. Why do you think people in the movies never watch TV or live in bland, boring apartments? Because it's too ordinary and uninteresting. Aristotle suggested in the *Poetics* that writers "choose what is impossible but plausible."

UNBELIEVABLY UNBELIEVABLE

The flip side of being too predictable is being too preposterous. Writers too often include events and situations that just wouldn't happen; they're not possible or plausible, given the characters and their situation.

Chris Meindl feels that in too many scripts he's read, "The plotting doesn't make sense, and to accept the leaps in logic the script makes, you have to be an idiot. Scripts need a clear, believable escalation of action and complications." The lack of logic is a complaint voiced repeatedly. As a studio analyst put it, "The plot needs to come out of character." That means that if you have a shy, retiring, church mouse of a character, they shouldn't suddenly force their way to the front of a line or perform a striptease for a hundred servicemen just because the plot needs it to happen. To be believable, the characters must experience something that will precipitate a change of behavior. Too often, according to David Weinstein, "Characters are cranked around so they'll work in the plot. The incongruities that result are ignored by the writer." When you outline, or write your first draft, ask yourself if the events flow logically and if the actions are believable.

If you're not completely confused by now between making things unpredictable and yet logical, there's one more aspect to consider. Once you're sure you're on solid ground and operating in the real world in your screenplay, you should stretch logic a little. Movie stories and characters are *somewhat* bigger than life. In addition to being realistic and unpredictable, your characters and the situations they face must also be cinematic and enjoyable. So, stretch everything to a slightly larger size, while retaining a realistic base. Think of *The Fugitive*. This is a story about real people, yet everything is heightened, ratcheted up a notch from mundane reality. It is movie reality, which means it's not quite real.

SOMETHING'S HAPPENING HERE

What it is ain't exactly clear. If your screenplay's confusing, you are in trouble. Robin Campbell finds that writers often don't "set things up properly." That doesn't mean everything has to be spelled out by page 5. We need to be curious about the people in the film and the problems they're going to face, but it's important that there is no confusion about which character is the hero and what problem he faces.

In *Chinatown*, both the audience and Jake Gittes were confused about what was really happening, and we didn't know much about the mysterious Mrs. Mulray or Noah Croft. But we knew that it was Gittes in the tree getting rocks thrown at him. We also knew that Mulray and Croft held some of the keys to the solution Gittes was looking for.

MISSING IN ACTION

Many writers turn in terrific first acts. They've got a story idea, and they lay it out in act one. After that, they're stuck. Randy Schmidt comments that, "After the first act set-up, too many writers flip-flop around for the next sixty pages." Jana Carole, a story analyst at Columbia, agrees, "Quite often, a script opens with a strong first act, but the writer never figures out where to go with it after that."

Having a well-defined through line that runs from the beginning of the story to the end will help. Allan Page suggests, "Be sure the primary thing driving the plot doesn't lose its weight and its centrality in the story. Remember the plot complications you've started, and don't get confused midway through."

According to Ted Dodd, scripts need "differentiation between acts, with the stakes continually upped and the interest in the story refreshed." So in act two, don't meander. Develop a continual escalation of tension, of conflict, and of pressure, until it seems the hero is down for the count. By outlining the story, you can map the through line and prevent getting lost in the wilderness of act two, while leading through the final crisis and resolution of act three.

Too Much Plot

While you want to make sure that your story has a smooth arc from beginning to end, and you don't want it to die in act two, you should also avoid including too many distracting scenes that contribute nothing to the ultimate outcome of the story. These scenes throw off the script's focus and forward movement. Make your story richer and more textured by developing a subplot or two. In *The Shawshank Redemption,* the stories of the warden and the young prisoner that Andy Dufresne tutored were full-blown subplots. Every scene was relevant to either the main story or the subplots.

Getting Help

One thing you should avoid is a concept that's been around since the Greeks wrote tragedies. Never solve tough script problems with a *deus ex machina.* No matter what corners you write yourself into, don't depend on God or his minions to get you out. Include no sudden appearance of elves, fairies, Satan, angels, a dead mother (unless you're rewriting *Fiddler on the Roof*), or landslides, a flood, a fire, or snow in July in the desert. You should avoid the sudden inclusion of anything completely unlikely whose only purpose is to help you out of a plot cul-de-sac.

Keeping It Internal

Keep the events in your story integral to the action. If in act three you introduce external elements to provide a new twist in your story, the reader or viewer is bound to wonder where they came from and recognize them as a weak solution to a plot problem. Plot twists should develop from the elements that have been previously introduced.

PLOT HOLES

They say that every script has a hole or two in it. Even *The Big Sleep*, the classic Humphrey Bogart film, has an unsolved murder. However, that doesn't mean you should ignore the unanswered questions in your script. If you let characters disappear, or if events don't tie into the main plot, the reader and the story's characters must have some explanation. That doesn't mean your story has to have a happy ending, it just means that all the plots and subplots must complete their dramatic arc. *Little Voice* is a good example. The mother and the agent don't succeed in exploiting the daughter as they had hoped, and the girl doesn't overcome her shyness and oddity. It isn't a completely happy resolution, but it doesn't leave the audience without an understanding of these characters' subsequent actions.

STARTING TOO SOON

Many writers start their scenes too early, spending too much time setting them up instead of focusing on the meat or the purpose the scene serves. For example, the opening scene of *The Ref* follows a guy in the middle of cracking a safe. It doesn't start with him 1) growing up and going bad, 2) explaining to the audience that he's a burglar, 3) casing the house, or 4) arriving in this small town. It doesn't even begin with him getting dressed for the robbery, crawling in the window, or taking out his tools. It begins on the action that is crucial to the outcome of the scene—the robbery, which is botched by a secret alarm inside the safe, necessitating that the robber hide out. Starting in the middle of the action is preferable to a lengthy scene setup. There's even a term for it. It's called *in medias res*, Latin for "in the middle of." That's where you want to start your story and each of your scenes. So, after you write your scenes, go back and see if you can't simply eliminate some of the opening lines and descriptions from them.

GETTING IT RIGHT

A well-crafted screenplay has three good acts, but it's not easy to write them all equally well. One reader felt that no one gets every act right. If a writer can write two good acts, that's a respectable achievement.

Here's a read-and-clip suggestion: Act one introduces the reader to the characters, their environment, and the story's primary conflict. This act is most often cited as the one that must dazzle readers. Many producers and development people who don't have to write coverage will simply stop reading if the first act or the first ten pages don't intrigue them.

In act two, you start mixing in complications. The action gets tenser, your hero can't possibly prevail, the subplots thicken, and the characters reveal more of themselves. Most of the readers surveyed felt that the hardest act to write is the second, because it's real drudge work. Often writers find it's easier to divide act two into two subacts, each about thirty pages long, with a miniclimax ending the first section. The second section continues the escalation of tension and action, culminating in the second-act climax.

The finale includes the climax of all the conflicts that started brewing in act one. The hero prevails in one way or another and will never be quite the same, the subplots get tied up, (if they aren't already), and the questions raised by the script are answered by the conclusion of act three.

CHARACTER AND DIALOGUE

Character is the story's centerpiece that communicates your premise and forces the plot to move forward. People go to the movies to see people solving problems or fulfilling a need. As Robin Campbell said, "No one wants to see movies about the Grand Canyon. They want to see movies about people in the Grand Canyon." Feature films, television movies-of-the-week, and television series are about people. If they weren't, we wouldn't watch them. Even in science fiction, the characters must behave in ways we recognize as human, or the meaning of the stories and our interest in them will be lost. We may love our dogs, but unless we can describe their behavior in anthropomorphic terms, we can't relate to them.

"Character is all there is to it. It is 100 percent of the job. What people care about is 'who is this happening to,' not 'what is happening,'" according to one of the reader's surveyed. All stories are driven by a central hero or protagonist. The audience must be able to relate to these characters. Occasionally, movies are made about a group of people, such as *Swingers* or *Election*, but even in these movies, one character takes prominence, and it is his or her story on which we focus.

To create characters that will be well-regarded by Hollywood, there are some essentials to remember.

GET REAL

Your characters must strike the reader as real and true to life. Analysts need to feel the character could actually exist. One way to achieve this, as one analyst said, is to "steal from real life. It always helps if a character is based on a real person. That way, you can't go wrong."

When you base your characters on people you have known, or on an amalgam of different people you have known, you'll avoid creating stereotypical characters. Stereotypes are the bane of development people. These characters have no personality, no individuality, in short, they have no felt life. They are abstractions of groups that society or sociologists or the media have labeled in a particular fashion. They are always spoiled rich boys, thugs, mob bosses, bigots, poor white trash, grandmas, etc. Avoid writing types, even in your minor characters. Although we may all match parts of a stereotypical pattern, no one is so lacking in individual needs and quirks that they are nothing more than the sum total of a stereotypical abstraction.

Occasionally a character in your story is an N.D. (i.e., no dialogue) and serves only as a functionary, such as a waiter or a gas station attendant. There is no need to describe these characters. But any character who has dialogue and appears in even one or two scenes should be given at least a little personality.

Children are the hardest characters to write. People who aren't around them, and even some that are, often reveal their ignorance of children when they create characters under eighteen. A recent script revolved around a six-year-old. In one scene, the child was coloring and making a mess of his mother's room, in the next, he was advising an adult character, spelling words, and dunking a basketball. If you don't have a child or aren't around a child the age of your story's character, then you need to do some research. Watch them. See what levels of maturity they generally exhibit at various ages. Find out how evolved their psychomotor skills are at different ages. Listen to their vocabulary. Don't assume because the children you have seen on TV are intellectually, socially, or sexually sophisticated that all children are. Children in sitcoms are notoriously unrealistic. Don't make assumptions about the behavior of children from different socioeconomic levels, races, or ethnic groups than your own. If you're writing a child into your script, find out what the real-life varieties are like.

Here's the secret exception to the suggestion that realistic characters are the ideal. Movie people aren't really duplicates of the real people you bump into every day. Although they must appear to be real people, they are only real within the context of the story. As with almost everything in the movies, reality is pushed a bit. Harrison Ford may be presented as an ordinary guy in *Witness*, but he's actually a little bigger than life. Real guys don't use their fists, their wit, their inner resources, their physical prowess, or their charm with such regularity or with quite the same high rate of success as movie heroes do.

LAYER IT ON

The most interesting characters in screenplays are those who are the most complex. Their personalities can't be summed up in a word or two. They have their own quirks, their own ways of approaching each action in life, from talking to a clerk in a store to talking to the president, from putting on their clothes to washing their face to walking down a hallway. From their views on life to their opinions of events around them, your characters, most assuredly your protagonist, should exhibit some texture and layering. The reader or viewer should not know everything about the hero at the end of page 1. There has got to be revelation as the story progresses.

In addition to creating an overall personality, Kim Ohanneson suggests that "writers should include not just the broad beats of a character arc, they should also include the little nuances of character." And "give them bits of business" to help assure they'll come alive on the page.

The most fully-realized characters in movies come into the story with their own background. They weren't born the minute they appear on screen. They have already lived some and had some character-forming experiences. Back story is the history of your plot and the biography of your main characters before the story opened. The characters' histories will determine how they will face the conflict you're going to throw at them.

To create this full-bodied, fully-operational individual, you need to, in the words of a senior vice president of development, "give your characters a lot of thought." And then, as David Weinstein suggests, "make explicit and detailed character notes" before you begin writing the screenplay. Write the biographical back story. Write a physical description. Write the basic facts of the character's life: What kind of home did he grow up in? How much schooling did he have? What kind of neighborhood did he live in? How did the family relate to one another? Write of the important events that have befallen the character over the years. Describe what opinions the character holds. Know your character inside and out. You're the god here. You're creating your Adam. Breathe the breath of life into him.

GETTING YOUR CHARACTER IN SYNCH

Once you've gotten a clear understanding of your protagonist, you must make sure that his speech and conversational style is consistent with the personality you've created. The character's behavior and actions must also work in harmony with his given personality. For example, if you've described a highly nervous, agitated person, it's unlikely that they would stroll slowly or stay calm in a crisis.

WHAT'S MY MOTIVATION

If you've got your protagonist and the other major characters clearly delineated, you've completed an important step. Now, you've got to supply them with adequate motivation. In your story, the protagonist is going to be faced with a problem that must be resolved. People are going to keep throwing rocks. The reader must understand why the hero keeps fighting his way through this crisis. In *The Fugitive*, the motivation is clear and quite simple. The man has been accused of a crime, and he needs to vindicate himself. In *Sleepless in Seattle*, the motivation is not so obvious. The heroine follows a feeling that she's meant for (and a desire to get married to) a particular man. The reader also has to believe that the protagonist has an investment in the outcome of the problem, other-wise, why would he get involved? As a director of development said, "I like characters who have a stake in their own fate. Passive characters who simply let things happen to them don't work."

Whatever the character's motivation, the audience has to believe the conflict or problem itself is important and worth the hero's time and trouble. In *Music from the Heart*, the lead character wants to rediscover herself and improve the possibilities and opportunities for her students. In *Erin Brockovich*, the protagonist wants to right what she feels is a moral and legal wrong, as well as gain some respect for herself and others.

CONSISTENTLY INCONSISTENT

Here's another one of the curves that's thrown at writers. While story editors and analysts tell you that characters need to behave in accordance with the personality they've been given, they still want to meet characters that surprise them occasionally. They don't want them to be too boringly consistent, because it isn't realistic or interesting. In real life, a person may truly believe in a certain principle or mode of behavior, but be blind to the fact that he violates that principle occasionally. Your protagonist's actions shouldn't contradict the limits of the personality you've assigned him, but sometimes he needs to react to situations in unexpected ways. For example, if your protagonist is a detective who doesn't believe in breaking and entering because it's illegal, then he does it anyway, it can be explained that breaking and entering was the only means possible to obtain some crucial information. Or the hero can charmingly admit that he doesn't take his own pronouncements too seriously. By avoiding stultifyingly consistent behavior, your characters become more interestingly human and endearing to an audience. And as Jana Carole said, "It is of the utmost importance that the audience have an emotional involvement with the characters on the screen."

CHEERING THEM ON

In most Hollywood films, we sympathize with the hero. Although there are those filmmakers who hate this formulaic approach and insist that audiences will come to see movies that feature complex, but not necessarily sympathetic characters, the majority of movies released feature a protagonist that the audience can root for. It doesn't mean that your lead character has to be a Dudley Doright or an unblemished all-American hero. Even in the realistic *Affliction*, Nick Nolte's character was far from noble, and he wasn't even very bright. Nonetheless, we rooted for his redemption and hoped he would triumph over the "afflictions" he suffers because of his father's abuse. Chris Meindl says that "you must start with a character who is likable to the audience, and by the end, he must even be more likable, while in the process you take him through hell and test everything he stands for." Unless you're sure you can pull off what Robert Altman did in *Short Cuts* or Paul Verhoven did in *Basic Instinct*, you are safer with characters that can engage an analyst or producer's sympathy.

GETTING STARS OUT OF YOUR EYES AND INTO YOUR MOVIE

We can discuss all the high-minded concepts about character from now till the turn of the next century, but there is a down-to-earth practical aspect to character. Writing characters we can root for is smart, but even smarter is writing characters that influential actors, otherwise known as stars, will be interested in playing. Actors want to play interesting people, people of action and determination, complex people. They don't want to play stereotypes, passive people who let life run over them, two-dimensional people, or people who have no emotions what-so-ever. This may even apply to current action films. Think of how much more fun Jackie Chan is than, say, several of the superaction heroes who preceded his domination of the box office. Making your protagonist appealing to prominent actors is reason enough for creating the best character you're capable of creating. There are actors in Hollywood who can get movies made.

SHOWING, NOT TELLING

When you finish creating your protagonist and the characters that surround him, and you're sure you understand them all inside and out, you've got to put them on the page and let the reader get to know them.

Analysts and producers prefer that we get to know characters through their actions. As Jana Carole said, "We don't learn a lot by what a character says, but how what they do relates to what they say." Most readers and development people agree that writing a lot of descriptive background is the least effective way to reveal character. Dialogue is a better approach, and the best way to disclose character is through action and what the character chooses not to say.

TALKING PICTURES

Film is a visual medium, and pure cinema is often defined as film with no sound. In this medium, unlike theater, dialogue always takes second place to the pictures on the screen. As an analyst said regarding dialogue, "Hitchcock said, write the screenplay and then add the dialogue. That's a visual story." She felt that writers should include no dialogue in their scripts until they've written at least eighty pages. Then they should go back and add what they need.

However, dialogue has been a constant in films since the early 1930s, and as David Weinstein said, "There are wonderful possibilities that can be achieved through dialogue, although most people ignore them in favor of action."

Whichever point of view you favor, you might find it reassuring to know that writing dialogue is one of the hardest skills to master. In fact, many analysts and producers are convinced that writing good dialogue is, above all else in screenwriting, dependent on natural talent or a natural ear for language. According to Jana Carole, "Dialogue is one of the things people have a knack for or not. It's a difficult thing to teach."

Obviously you want the dialogue you write to aid your script rather than tip the scales against it. To help you achieve that goal, there are some essentials that you should keep in mind as you write.

SOUNDING NATURAL

Dialogue must sound natural, although it doesn't duplicate ordinary human speech. It is "movie natural," or, as a director of development said, "Real-life dialogue is often too slow-moving and dull." So, the natural-sounding dialogue in movies is really spiffed up and tailored for the context.

As a reader for a large studio said, the reality of dialogue depends on the style of the piece. "You establish the reality of the script, and in that context, dialogue needs to fit naturally." Chris Meindl goes even farther: "There's movie dialogue, real dialogue, and quasi-real movie dialogue. Movie dialogue is altogether different from real dialogue, but it must strive to sound real even though it's mannered to fit the context. In real dialogue, we hem and haw, repeat ourselves, stumble around, etc. Quasi-real movie dialogue tries too hard to sound real, and it doesn't succeed." Although film dialogue should fall within the general dimensions of natural human speech, it doesn't actually match it. Here again, movies push reality a bit with dialogue that has the gloss of reality, while actually, it can't operate outside the movie for which it's written.

In real life, people often don't speak in complete sentences. Your characters shouldn't either. In real life, people are often elliptical—they understand each other with common code words and signs. Your characters should follow suit. People rarely pontificate for minutes on end. Your characters shouldn't engage in any long-winded speeches either. There is another reason for avoiding long speeches. As Ted Dodd said, "In the industry, long dialogue doesn't get read." Most important, don't let your characters imitate the movies. As Robin Campbell explained, "Too many characters sound like what the writer thinks people in the movies sound like."

In real life, people usually aren't direct. They rarely express exactly what they're thinking or feeling. When it's done in the movies, it's called being on-the-nose. It's too literal, and it isn't natural, since in real life, most of our conversations are oblique. To understand how dialogue dances around issues without confronting them, watch the great American theatrical classic *Long Day's Journey into Night* by Eugene O'Neill.

BY CRACKIE OR BY JOVE

Dialogue must fit the era in which your film is set. If you write a movie about colonial times, you won't have a character squealing, "Cool, dude." That's an obvious example, but you get the idea. It's difficult to know how people actually spoke before recordings were made, and even if you did duplicate it, no one could understand what your characters were saying. The best approach is to modify the dialogue so it gives the general impression that it is speech that might be heard in the era of your story. You will also need to avoid any contemporary slang or neologisms that have recently been added to the language. Masterpiece Theatre often features pieces that are masterful at catching the sense of earlier eras without actually attempting to replicate the speech of those times.

WE TALK ALIKE

One of the biggest complaints that analysts have is that all the characters in scripts sound alike. As Jana Carole said, "One sign of a novice is even if the writer has a way with dialogue, all the characters sound alike, which is like the writer." Cover up the names of your characters in your script. If you can't tell which one is speaking, then you need to work on individualizing your characters' voices.

According to Ted Dodd, "Very few people can create characters who come from a particular background and make them sound real." Writing your character descriptions should help you write the dialogue. For Kim Ohanneson, "Doing a lot of character work beforehand will help the writer find the voices." Once you have those characters firmly in mind and see them as individuals, then appropriate dialogue should flow out of them as naturally as it does out of the people you meet in your everyday life.

In your character biographies, you should include the person's background, level of education, how they view themselves, what kinds of jobs they have, and what milieu they travel in. All these things will help you individualize their speech.

MOVING RIGHT ALONG

David Weinstein spoke for many analysts when he said, "The goal of the dialogue is to further the plot and develop character." There isn't much reason, and there certainly isn't enough time to dawdle about with unnecessary speeches. As Frank Balkin suggested, "Every word that's spoken should be there for a purpose. If it doesn't either further the plot or reveal character, lose it!" You have to be tough on yourself. Even if you've written something you think is charming and cute, if it doesn't serve any purpose, the reader will wonder why it's there. Anything that stops action will be noticed and noted.

YAWN

Asked what her biggest complaint was about dialogue, an analyst at Warner Bros. said, "Clichéd and flat." An executive also said, "Leaden and flat." It's a complaint that was echoed by several others. You know dialogue has to sound natural and specific to a character and that it has to move things forward. Well, now you know that it also needs to be interesting. One analyst said that "most of the time dialogue is barely functional. It needs to have some wit and sparkle. It needs to have some weight or punch." Good dialogue was once described as walking in one door, but instead of going straight through out the opposite door, it takes an abrupt left turn and goes out the side door. Just as each scene contains its own arc, so, too, does dialogue. By the end of the scene, the dialogue should be other than where it was expected to be when the scene began. To wit: Dialogue needs to be interesting, surprising, and to keep the reader off guard by taking unexpected turns.

LESS REALLY IS MORE

When it comes to dialogue, most analysts agree with Laura Glendinning that less is more. The less dialogue that's used, the more powerful each speech will be. Robin Campbell urges writers to "be brief. No one wants long rhetorical speeches. Be honest, but make every line count." One way you can be economical with your dialogue is to follow the advice of Allan Page, "Don't let your dialogue be redundant to action." In other words, if you can see it, you don't need to say it.

How, then, can you adhere to all these injunctions about dialogue? Analysts and producers have a few tips.

The first and most often repeated advice is to listen. Jana Carole suggests writers "listen to the diversity of voices" that surround each of us. "Sit at lunch counters and listen." Chris Meindl adds, "As well as anything else, the role of the writer is to listen."

When you listen, you might also take another suggestion from Meindl, "When people say something interesting, clever, funny, or striking, write it down. Or when you read something terrific, cut it out. Record people. Eavesdrop on conversations."

One exercise that is a great help to many writers is to read your dialogue out loud. Reading it, according to Frank Balkin, will help you be sure "it sounds like human beings speaking." Another suggestion is to get a group of actors to read your work. Hearing it can be enlightening, and you will see immediately which lines don't work when spoken rather than written. It isn't an easy experience to endure, but it will be worth it.

A FEW FINAL NOTES

9

"In Italy for thirty years under the Borgias, they had warfare, terror, murder, and bloodshed, and they produced Michelangelo, Leonardo de Vinci, and the Renaissance. In Switzerland, they had brotherhood and five hundred years of democracy and peace, and what did they produce? The cuckoo clock."

There are other things about writing for Hollywood that you'll need to be cognizant of and learn how to use to aid your pursuit of success as a film writer. These have nothing to do with writing, but are ways to give yourself some additional leverage and survive with your ego intact in what is considered by all to be a bruising, rude, highly-competitive business that too often believes in its own myths rather than in its realities.

NOT A WORD ABOUT THIS TO ANYONE

LET'S GET PRACTICAL

One of the best things you can do for yourself if you're serious about pursuing your dreams of success in Hollywood is to move to Los Angeles. Wait. Don't start reciting all the crap you hear about dangerous L.A.; earthquake-toppled L.A.; spread-out, freeway-dependent L.A.; pollution-racked L.A. Ignore all that stuff. Are most of the things they say about your hometown true? The same goes for Los Angeles. You know how the media, by just doing its job, inadvertently creates pictures of cities, groups of people, and entities that simply aren't the *whole* story. What you need to know about Los Angeles is that this is where it's happening as far as movies and television are concerned. Every state hopes to lure moviemaking to their turf, and lots of pictures are made outside Los Angeles County. But the business is done here. The scripts are bought here. The planning is done here. And, until that changes, here is the place to be.

There is a common wisdom heard around this town that says that you have to stay in Los Angeles until you "make it," then you can move anywhere you want. The assumption is that after your first serious success, or string of small successes, you'll have the contacts you need, you'll have an agent who will work for you, and you'll be able to afford frequent trips back to keep abreast of the business. Until that happens, you need to get into the belly of the beast.

WE SAID IT BEFORE

It can't be said too often. Every script analyst and producer recommends that writers who want to succeed read, and read, and read some more. This should include books, screenplays, newspapers, magazines, the classics, just about everything.

KEEPING YOUR EDGE

An assistant who had just gotten his first job in the industry asked a development executive how he could get to know the who, what, where, and how of the industry as fast as possible. The executive told him, "Read the trades." You, too, should keep informed of what's going on in the industry. Do it by talking to people, keeping in touch with your contacts, and by reading industry newspapers. The popular magazines such as *Premiere* and *Entertainment Weekly* are good, but you need more than magazines for entertainment buffs. You should subscribe to either or both *Daily Variety* and the *Hollywood Reporter*—either the hard copy or the online version. These two dailies let you know who's bought whom— companies, that is—what producers have signed new contracts, how many films given production companies are planning, the establishment of new production companies and what kinds of films they want to do, the box office results of the latest movies, the ratings of current television shows, and much more about the business. A few months later, that new assistant used to amaze some of his coworkers and bosses with his knowledge of the industry, when all he had done was read the trades.

With the advent of the Internet, there are dozens of sites dedicated to Hollywood gossip, information, news, and celebrity watching. While some of these are good, others offer little more than extreme fan fare. Depending on your interest, check out all that interest you. But for solid, dependable, industry information, you can depend on the two long-established dailies.

WHAT'S A BEST BOY?

If you're planning to work in this industry selling more scripts than you can imagine, it is wise to know as much as you can about the process of making movies. As one writer said, "The more understanding you have of the crafts, the more you enhance your chance to succeed." You ought to know something about acting, editing, cinematography, and line production. Anything you learn will help you become a knowledgeable professional.

P.O. BOXES AND OTHER FAKERY

If you really can't come to Los Angeles, not even for awhile, then the next best thing is to create the appearance of living in the city. Whether they admit it or not, when most readers see an out-of-county or out-of-state address on a script, they unconsciously assume the script will be less than professional. This assumption is correct often enough to confirm their fears. If you have a friend who lives in Los Angeles that will accept mail for you, use that friend's address. If you don't know anyone who lives in the area, rent a post office or private box. Some private box companies use a street address and a suite number instead of a box number. It makes it sound like an office or an apartment rather than a mailbox.

CONTACTS

Don't you hate this word? It has definitely overstayed its welcome. Yet, it's still with us. Networking is one of those concepts that everyone grabs onto for dear life, as if it's the answer to everything. It isn't. Too often, it creates an image of people trying to meet dozens and dozens of people, not because they like people, enjoy the same career, want to find someone to love, want to find others whose passion for a particular career or art they share, but because they want to further themselves, i.e., use other people, if they can. I don't think networking always plays out that way in reality, yet to hear some people talk, you would think people are merely stones to step on in their desperate search for achievement.

Finding others whose company you like and whose passions you share is probably more difficult for writers than it is for performers. Writers' work is isolating and solitary. They don't have to be at the theater at three to rehearse with a half dozen other people—all of whom they'll learn to like or dislike. In Los Angeles, sidewalk cafes or bars where people are regulars and speak freely to each other and to newcomers just don't exist. Because they're locked up by themselves all day talking to a word processor, lots of writers probably don't have their socializing skills in top form. (Why do you think writers drink? All that aloneness makes you ache for company.) You have to make a point of getting to know people. Lots of people.

Take some classes at U.C.L.A. or U.S.C. or any other Los Angeles college that offers film courses. Talk to people at the gym, at the supermarket, join a club, learn to play tennis, get involved in politics. Do stuff that will get you in touch with other people. Some or maybe lots of people will be involved in the business. Take a temporary job at a studio. Do scut work for subcontractors, like optical houses or editing shops or whatever you can. You'll meet some people. If, like some of the young writers in Los Angeles, you went to U.C.L.A. or U.S.C., you've got an advantage. Not only are you friends of and know other ex-students, lots of people in the industry are alums of those schools.

AT LEAST KEEP IT WARM

When you make a contact in this town, keep it. The surprising thing about Hollywood is that you can call someone you haven't spoken to in a couple of years, and usually, they'll remember you. That's not necessarily true of agents or professionals who have huge numbers of people soliciting them, but if you've had a face-to-face positive encounter of more than a minute or two's duration with someone in the business, don't let that contact get away. If someone in the business encourages you, ask them if you can send them other material—and then do it. In all involvements in which you feel there is positive mutual regard, keep in touch.

A CLASS ACT

It is probably a good idea to take some classes in writing and film. Many new writers take classes to improve their writing and to feel like they are part of the scene. The American Film Institute offers classes. U.C.L.A. and U.S.C., both of which have film schools, have extensive programs covering all areas of the industry. There are also private classes held by professional industry people.

As you go along in your career, your need for these classes will lessen, but in the early years, they're very helpful. Being around others and talking about writing inspires you to get started on your own projects.

THE COMPANIES YOU KEEP

As you get apprised of the industry, you should pay special attention to those companies that produce the kinds of movies you write. Keep track of them: what they're doing, the new films they have coming down the pipeline, and if someone new comes in as head of production. Keep your finger on their pulse for your own good.

TO MARKET TO MARKET

Never let yourself forget that making movies is a commercial enterprise, and by writing for the movies, you are one kind of commercial writer. Your stories can have depth, feeling, searing human emotions, blinding truths, and ageless profundity. And that's good. But don't forget you have to sell it.

BEING A SCRIPTWRITER

WORKING

In many ways, it's easier to practice your craft if that craft involves other people—like actors and editors and wardrobe people. As a writer, no one is dependent on you to show up to do the job. As a consequence, it's easy to procrastinate. If you're writing on spec, it means there is no deadline, and no one is waiting for the pages. You can put off writing until you bite it. Freelance writing probably takes more discipline than any other profession, at least until someone is willing to pay for your services and you are forced to get yourself going every morning just to meet a deadline.

One way to coerce yourself into writing is to get a partner. When you cowrite, you have to meet with that person and prepare your share of the material. It's a motivating force that's very effective, as long as you get along with your partner and your points of view about material are identical, or they mesh or complement each other, or each partner is willing to capitulate on some points.

More often than not, however, you will write on your own. Many writers swear by having an office or a space away from their home—even if it's the guest room over the garage. That becomes your work space. If you can't afford to actually rent an office or have a space separate from where you live, you still must arrange an area in your home that is your "office." A highly-successful writer suggests that you set yourself a schedule that's consistent each week, then every day, get yourself up, get dressed as you would if you were going to an outside job, and arrive at your desk at the appointed time. Then, work on the projects you are currently writing. If you establish this routine, you'll begin to feel like a writer, even if you haven't sold anything. The ritual itself creates a sense of purpose and belonging.

IT'S HARD WORK

Writing for the movies is one of the most difficult professions at which to succeed. Keep that in mind when the rejection letters and returned scripts start filling your mailbox. All writing jobs are competitive, difficult to get, most are low-paying, and there's little or no net gain in the numbers of jobs available. For every writing job created in one sector, it seems jobs are lost in another.

Because of the possibility of a high payoff, lots of people are drawn to screenwriting, and that's why it is littered with people who have realized they have to pay to play. Even experienced people who have already sold scripts have a tough time setting up each subsequent project.

FOLLOW THE MONEY

If you want to be a doctor or a psychiatrist, you know before you start that you won't be hanging out a shingle for probably ten years. You have to spend a lot of time in school and pay a lot of dues. After you get through, you'll probably earn a pretty good living doing something you love. Despite all the stories you hear, being a scriptwriter is very similar to becoming a doctor. It takes a long time to learn the craft, make connections, get through a lot of failed attempts, and survive rejection before your phone starts ringing with offers. Then, you'll probably be able to make a pretty good living. Keep in mind that newspapers don't write dog-bites-man stories, they write man-bites-dog stories. The news reports of multimillion-dollar script sales are featured in newspapers because they are man-bites-dog tales.

If you get hired on a television show as a writer, your income will be very comfortable for as long as the series airs. After it ends, you go looking for another gig. Providing you sell a screenplay for a considerable amount over the minimum, you can live comfortably for awhile. Still, you have to realize that you may not make another sale (despite dozens of meetings and promises) for another two, three, or five years. So, if you thought that writing scripts was an easy road to riches, think again. It's a tough, time-consuming road that may never lead to a bank balance that can finance a life of ease. If you're in it for the money, there are easier ways to make your fortune—real estate, neurosurgery, politics, illegal drugs. You probably will be very disappointed by the net return on your investment in this business.

When a Screenplay Isn't a Screenplay

There is a saying that luck is being ready when the opportunity presents itself. If you have to sub for the star, it won't be a lucky break if you don't know the dance routine. In the same way, if you've got a lot of incomplete scripts lying around, or some unfinished first acts, you don't have a script. And when you meet someone who's looking for the kind of project you've got in your mind but not on paper, and they say "send it" or "let me see it," you won't be ready. Being a professional isn't just about talking a good game, it's about doing it, finishing it, following it through.

Passion and All That

Writing isn't all passion and inspiration. Feeling so strongly about something that you have to write about it is passion. That's about 10 percent of the task. The other 90 percent is taking that idea and developing it, working it out, and writing a full, complete story from it. Why do you think successful producers hire writers to work out their movie ideas? Because it's the hard part. If you stop working on a project when the obsession begins to lose its magic, it could mean the difficulty of working out mundane story problems overwhelms you. How will you get anywhere if you're not willing to work something through to the finish—the easy and the hard parts?

Be Virginal

No matter how many times you've been rejected, you have to start each new project as if it were your first. With each new story, you must exude the same enthusiasm you had for your initial offering. You must possess the certainty that this time out, you will knock 'em dead.

NEVER SIMPLIFY

Thoreau exhorted us to simplify. He did not mean scripts. Writing a sixty-page hour-long or a 120-page screenplay is no simple feat. Analysts, who as a group read more bad scripts than anyone else in Hollywood, continue to admire the fact that people take the time and effort to work out a 120-page story and then write it. It's not simple. It's commendable. Similarly, don't simplify mastering the craft. You won't be able to do it in a week or a month or probably not even a couple of years.

UNPLUGGED

There are times when you will get blocked. Nothing comes to mind, and what leaks out is seaweed—soggy and shapeless. You can't seem to get anywhere. It's okay. Writer's block happens to everyone somewhere along the line. Don't baby yourself too much. Don't allow yourself to stop just because there's a difficult plot turn coming up. On the other hand, if you're in the middle of that plot turn and suddenly, or slowly, none of the words you write seem to do anything but hang on the page like a smeared fingerprint, stop for awhile. Take a break, go bowling, see a movie, do anything to get away from the material. You'll come back to it renewed and ready to begin again. And if you don't, picture yourself flipping burgers at McDonald's. That should get you restarted.

IT'S AN EGO THING

Practically every day in Hollywood, you can find ways to make yourself feel bad. If you aren't hearing the latest success story, you're reading about it. If you aren't getting a rejection, your phone calls aren't answered. If people aren't asking you in so many words when you're going to do something important with your life, they're wondering how insane you are to live without a regular income. To counter these assaults, learn to keep your spirits up and your goals focused.

HOLLYWOOD GAMES

There is a roar in Los Angeles, and it isn't the sound of the freeways. What you hear is mostly Hollywood bull dung. Remember the scene in *The Big Picture* in which Kevin Bacon's character meets up with his nemesis, who's got three deals set up around Hollywood and is about to begin another? Bacon asks him, "How's that cure for cancer coming?" It seems like the guy has everything going for him, he knows everything, and what's more everything's going so right, it's scary. There are always people in the business that seem to be doing everything. If you don't run into them personally, you read about them in the trades, or see them on *Entertainment Tonight,* or the *Los Angeles Times* oozes about their many, many simultaneous accomplishments in a front page "L.A. Times Calendar" story.

You've got to remember that the person being written about has undoubtedly had his bad times and probably will have them again. Also, when you condense several events into one story, as is often done for publication, it compacts life in an unrealistic manner. In reality, the deals may not be complete, the actual contracts read far differently than publicists want us to believe, and in Hollywood, individuals and their managers and agents learn quickly that the appearance of success begets more success. So, everyone who has even a little success is promoted as the most talented entertainer or artist since William Shakespeare. Don't worry about these stories. Stop reading them for awhile if they depress you too much. Your turn will come.

Put Up or Shut Up

There are people in this town who would have you believe that they have done nothing since birth but write scripts. No matter how many scripts you have, they've written more. No matter what topic is brought up, they've written a script about it. These people have a lot of time to go to parties, schmooze over long lunches, and hang out. Lots of people think that if they have thought about a script idea, made notes on a script idea, written the first three pages or the first act of a script idea, they have written a script. They haven't. It's difficult to be kind to these people. Try calling their bluff by expressing great interest in one or several of their scripts, and ask to see them. Ten to one, you'll never see it.

This Takes Skill?

There are those times when the brain-dead son of a celebrity sells a script for enough money to start his own country. The story, as described in three sentences in the trades, sounds like the most preposterous notion you've heard since the girl across the aisle from you in first grade told you her real mother is Mother Theresa.

There's the story of a studio that hired two young men from out of town for thirteen weeks at $1,000 a week based on a story idea they had. It seems impossible, but it happens. Unlike education or the law or accounting, Hollywood isn't about credentials, it's about selling. If you can sell yourself or your product, you're in. The part worth remembering is that if you can't perform once you're in, like the two young men, you're back out. Always take stories like the one above with a large block of salt. These tales go through so many people that it's like a game of gossip at a slumber party—whatever comes out at the end of the line bears little resemblance to the original, true story.

DEADLY ENCOURAGEMENT

There's a trap you can get caught in if you don't keep your own counsel. In Hollywood, no one likes to be discouraging, because one person's dreck might be another's manna. To be on the safe side, they say something nice rather than nothing at all. You can't let yourself be overly influenced by these casually-impersonal words of kindness. As Oscar Wilde said, "It's so easy to be kind to those we care nothing about." Be ruthless with yourself. Be your own worst critic. Careless encouragement can be a killer if it keeps you at something for which you have no real inclination.

KEEPIN' IT TO YOURSELF

As you get more into life as a scriptwriter in Los Angeles, you'll start acting, talking, and thinking like movie people. If this happens, you might lose your own particular vision of the world, and with it will go your ability to create fresh characters and stories. You'll start thinking in terms of stereotypes. You will pursue hipness, hang out at the right places, drive the right status car, wear the right clothes, support the politically-correct causes, and use the current slang. Your personal vision of life, the one you grew up with, the real you, will be gone. If this starts happening, it's time to take a break from Hollywood and recapture your own point of view.

APPRECIATION

It is said that the need to be appreciated is as indigenous to the human character as the need for food and shelter. Taking up the life of a struggling Hollywood writer will afford you very little appreciation of your talents for some time. Until you break through, you will have to suffer rejection and disinterest. Nobody will be around to believe in you, unless you're lucky and come supplied with fans or an adoring spouse. Even then, you will ask yourself, "Do they really love my work, or are they just being kind?" Writing on spec is much easier if you get some positive feedback. Unfortunately, in your position as a struggling writer, very little praise comes your way. You may find it hard to get yourself going every day. The secret is this: You have to believe in yourself absolutely, or you won't make it.

No Apologies

If you've chosen this life, be confident of your convictions. Never apologize for not becoming a novelist, playwright, getting a Ph.D., or getting a real job. Don't apologize for not making money at it. Everyone in the arts complains about not making any money. They worry about money. They wish they had money. Yet, very few would trade what they are doing for a job selling insurance, working at a bank, or even getting on Microsoft's impressive payroll.

The Ten-Year Rule

Overnight success is a common myth that's perpetuated by Hollywood and the press. Everyone wants to believe that someone sat down to a word processor and a couple weeks later finished a script, then sold it for a million dollars two days later. When someone who's never sold a script before sells one for a sizable amount, the press and the publicists predictably peddle the same story they've been writing for years: The writer is always a first-timer and young. A teacher, a parent, or a producer along the line failed to see the genius's talent; and the writer plans to buy an expensive car. In reality, writers who sell a big script have generally already written several others before the one that sold. The writer's been around town for awhile learning the business and learning to write. And they are often older than their published age.

One analyst recounted the ten-year rule. When he first arrived in Los Angeles, an agent told him that the first ten years you starve, and then if things work well, you get a small foothold in the business. There are people who sell their very first script. There are people who do it in three or five or two years. Don't pin your hopes on the exceptions to the rule.

The other aspect of Hollywood that you must be aware of is the lack of upward career movement. If you join a company after college, you're expected to work your way to middle or upper management. At least the raises are regular. For creative people in Hollywood, it doesn't happen that way. You have to keep your wits about you and find your strength in yourself and your writing, not your title—which you don't have, or a hoped-for title, or an increasing premium on your screenplays—though you hope the amount you can command for your writing escalates.

STAYING SANE

Chris Meindl suggested that writers who want to succeed in this business should "remain humble and cognizant of the caprice of life, because the person who takes your restaurant order today could be the next Sidney Pollack, or the person you hang up on today might be the person you're pitching your project to tomorrow. It's always fascinating how this town works." According to Meindl, the best thing to do is "be nice, be modest, and keep a level head about yourself."

Don't forget the phrase heard around Hollywood: Every day you don't write, the bastards win.

FROM THE TOP

10

"So there it is."

Helping you get your script in its most presentable, most ideal, most salable form wouldn't be complete without a few words from the people who actually green-light projects: the producers and executives on whose desk land those scripts that analysts recommend, and writers who have successfully navigated the uncertain tides of Hollywood. Following then, as further guidance and insight for your work, are seven brief question-and-answer interviews with some of the most influential people working in the industry.

STEVE WHITE

Steve White, executive vice president for motion pictures, miniseries, and special projects at NBC Television, has overseen the development and production of dozens of films, including *A Wing and a Prayer, Operation Sandman, She Said No, The Rose,* and *The Jackal* for television, and the features, *The Devil's Advocate* and *The Adventures of Huck Finn.* Steve, one of the most personable, low-key executives in the business, succeeds more than most at getting movies made. He was formerly an independent producer and president of New World Pictures.

What's the first thing you notice when you begin a script?
I notice if the writing engages me. I either find myself involved or slipping off the page. There is a sense that the material is either alive or it

isn't. And by alive, I mean getting a feeling that this story could really be happening.

What is the most important script element for you?
Character. If the characters don't sound real, if they aren't real people, nothing can save the script.

What is the most common script problem you find?
Most often, I find two things: The inability to move the story forward quickly enough, and a slow or ponderous opening with too much descriptive prose that focuses on nonessential elements.

What type of film is the hardest to write?
Interpersonal character dramas, especially two-character ones, are the hardest, because it all hinges on who the characters are, and because it has to be so real. The most difficult thing to write is conflict that comes out of character.

What problems with developing plot do you see most often?
The best story is one where the plot stays one step ahead of the reader. Writers have a tendency to go back to the beginning and set everything up. But dramatically, a film really starts when the character has a reason to enter or there's an immediate conflict. Writers should try throwing out the first ten pages and see how the script reads.

Should scripts be written in three acts?
This is the classic three-act structure. If you don't have it, you don't have a beginning, middle, and end, and it's not a real drama. The concept of three acts comes from theater. The curtain falls at the end of each act. Television also has act breaks (for commercials). While feature films need them in structural terms, there isn't necessarily a clear distinction from one to the other.

Which is the most important act to get right?
That is like asking which is the most important part of the body, the head, the heart, or the legs. If you're missing any of them, you have a hard time getting around. They are all part of a whole.

How can writers know when their characters come alive on the page?
Characters saying the opposite of what you want them to say is a clear indication that the character is alive. If you really have characters that are alive, the biggest mistake you can make is to force them to say what you want them to say. When you do that, you lose their voices.

Any tips for writing dialogue?
Listen to your characters. The greatest thing to find is a character that speaks to you. Let them say what they want. The dialogue in too many scripts lacks originality, lacks a voice, uses too many well-worn phrases, and every character sounds alike.

Any suggestions for finding a premise or theme?
Choosing a premise is the hardest thing in the world. You have to have something to say, and it's got to be true to human experience.

How do you see your role in filmmaking?
A good producer finds and shapes projects. That shaping can be working with the material and with the people who are brought on the project, i.e., writers, directors, actors, etc.

Is the development process changing?
Yes, I think it is. It's much harder. There's been a swing toward scripts based on sensational media events. That's not necessarily good, but we'll start a swing back to telling good stories, in which writers play a bigger part.

Any last comments about scripts in general?
A good script is a good script is a good script. A good idea can't fix a bad script, and great characters with no story to tell can't make a good movie. You have to have good characters and a good story.

Any general advice for writers?
Find material that connects you to your inner creative drive. In other words if it turns you on, write about it. If it doesn't, don't write about it.

JOHN WARREN

John Warren started his career writing short stories, and after a stint in the American Film Institute Writing Program, he took up screenwriting and presently writes and directs. His insights as a writer-director who is very much aware of how the process works in Hollywood are some of the best around. He's often asked to read scripts for a possible rewrite. His work includes *Major League: Back to the Minors,* which he wrote and directed; the independent features, *The Girl in the Cadillac* and *Naked in New York,* and the television film, *August Fires.* He's also written hour-long episodes for television series.

What do you notice first about a script?
Structure. Too many new writers get caught in the romance of writing, of being writers. It's a mistake. Writers like these spend the first thirty pages purging. They explain their philosophy. They're not doing the business of setting up a story. They haven't told us the main idea, the motivation, the problem. When I see scripts like this, I know it will only get worse.

What is the most important script element for you?
Defining the main characters' motivations. That has a lot to do with the spine of the story and where it's going. What does the character want, and how much is he willing to pay. We'll follow a character if he's passionate. If the hero succeeds without sacrificing anything, it's not satisfying. It's not drama.

What script element turns you off?
If the motivation is too weak or implausible or the stakes aren't high enough. These things need to be clearly defined in a script.

What type of film is the hardest to write?
Probably the mystery, because the audience is less forgiving. When you say to an audience, "This is a mystery thriller," you're inviting them to beat you to the final revelation. And audiences are sophisticated. If anything doesn't work, they'll call you on it. The audience for comedy is more forgiving. They want to laugh, and if they do at all, they'll accept the shortcomings. In love stories, the audience is much more forgiving. They want to go along with it. But mysteries are a challenge to the audience, and the writer can't slip up, even once.

What is the most common script problem you see?
Writers are too kind to their main character. They don't make the hero go through enough. And the most obvious problem I see is writers who

start writing without knowing where they're going. They're so thrilled with the character, they just write. At eighty pages, all the horses are out of the barn, and they suddenly realize they have to get them back in the next thirty pages, but it's too late. They can't do it.

What do you think is the most important thing to consider when developing plot?
The films I like have nuance, some details that seem insignificant at the time, but in the third act, we find out it wasn't insignificant at all. That sort of thing lends credibility to the plot.

What common plot problems do you see in scripts?
Writers cheat. We all do. At the roughest point in the story, you need a motivation, so you find one that's not really satisfying and settle for it. At the time, it seems okay. Later you go back and realize it's bogus. It's not credible. You have to learn how to ask yourself the right questions about your script. If you can see problems, then you can work out a solution. You have to be sophisticated about story.

Any tips for writers with regard to plot?
See lots of movies. Watch how filmmakers have gone about telling their story. It's a very demanding craft, not a hit-or-miss one.

How about character?
Character follows story. It's a delicate trick to pull off, but character follows story.

What would you advise in terms of dialogue writing?
Dialogue is one of the few areas that can't be learned. You have to have an ear for speech. I don't think people develop it—it's a talent—but you can be successful without it.

Dialogue should sound real, but it isn't really. Everything is heightened, because two hours is a restrictive length of time.

Any advice for writers?
I know writers, particularly young ones, who are undisciplined. They think it's all born out of passion. It isn't. Passion emerges after the outline. I know lots of people with eighty-page, unfinished scripts, because they ran out of "passion."

You need to remember that writing is tedious and hard. Don't take the craft lightly. And don't assume you can just write. Keep practicing, and keep learning about the craft.

There are too many young writers who aren't in love with literature or films. They're looking for the glamour or the big score with killer money. If that's your motivation, you won't be able to gut it out.

LAWRENCE TURMAN

Since the early 1960s, Lawrence Turman has been producing some of the country's most important and most successful movies, either on his own or with a partner. Just a small sample of his pictures includes: *American History X, Mass Appeal, Running Scared, The Mean Season, The Great White Hope, The Graduate, The Drowning Pool,* and *The Best Man.* His latest is *What's the Worst That Could Happen?* He has also produced many television movies. His production company is currently based at MGM.

How does the development process work at your company?
We get scripts, we take pitches, and we solicit projects that we want to develop. We don't have any readers or development people on staff. I read the material I get myself.

What kinds of material do you favor?
I personally prefer material that is American, contemporary, and life-affirming.

What do you notice first as you begin a script?
I notice if it's well-written. That has no bearing on its commercial viability; it has no bearing on anything, but I look for quality writing.

What is the most important element of a script?
I simply ask myself, "Do I like it or not? Does it compel me to keep turning the pages?"

What is the most common script error you find?
I don't know that there is a common error. I wouldn't use the word error. It's presumptuous. It takes doing to sit down and write a script.

What is the hardest type of film to write?
I have no idea.

What problem with developing plot do you see most often?
A lack of clarity—who is doing what to whom and why.

What do you think is the most important thing for a writer to consider when developing plot?
Perhaps his or her own feelings and goals.

Do you think screenplays should be written in a three-act structure?
There are no "shoulds" in writing screenplays. Many people in Hollywood talk about the three-act structure, but I haven't seen a three-act play in a generation. They're all two acts.

      The three-act approach can be summarized as: act one, get someone in a tree; act two, throw rocks at him; act three, get him down.

Which is the most important act to get right?
All of them. The whole is made up of pieces. It has to become a whole.

What's your biggest complaint about dialogue?
Those times I don't like the dialogue, it's because I don't think it's good or true.

Any advice about writing dialogue?
No writer has ever asked me, nor should they.

What's the best way to make sure characters come alive in a script?
By having a wonderfully talented writer.

Any suggestions for finding a premise or theme?
It should come from within the writer.

Have you ever developed a screenplay that had a great premise or idea, but needed a new script written around it?
It is nearly always a losing proposition. Generally, people have ability or they don't.

How do you see your role in filmmaking?
A producer's function is to help the writer clarify or realize his or her theme, etc.

A producer is also an editor to everyone else, when required, although not in an interfering way.

A producer is that person who causes the picture to be made.

Any advice for writers?
Write and live; live and write. You should follow your own taste. And remember, to succeed in Hollywood, know and have your own center. I'm not being Zen; this is just what I feel.

NEIL RUSSELL

Neil Russell has been in the motion picture business for over twenty years. Beginning as a booker for Paramount Pictures, he's currently an independent producer. Quietly confident and straightforward, Neil embodies all the best qualities a Hollywood executive can have. Some of the films he has green-lighted include: *Donato and Daughter* for CBS, which he also executive produced; Judith Krantz's *Dazzle*, also for CBS; *Deadly Matrimony, House of Secrets, Desperate Rescue,* and *Murder Between Friends* for NBC; and *Cherynobl: The Final Warning* for TNT.

What is the first thing you notice when you begin a script?
The title. If a script has a good title, it gets my attention. Good titles pique interest and catch your eye. Untitled scripts are just the opposite. If a writer doesn't make the effort to put a title on it, why should I be interested?

What's the most important script element for you?
It depends on what we're looking for. If it's action, did the writer write good action? In that situation, we can beef up the characters. It's a balancing act. No one's good at every aspect of scriptwriting.

What do you look for in your projects?
I read closely for story. Is it compelling? Does it have a beginning, middle, and an end? The number and nature of characters can be enlarged or cut,

but if you start with a poor concept, you can't make it better with interesting characters. I look for good yarn spinners. Someone who can get your attention with a tale gets a big push here.

What is the most common script problem you find?
It's the same over and over. Writers consistently make the assumption that the reader has as much information as the writer. It usually happens on the first page or in the set-up. The writer doesn't establish clearly where he or she is or where the story is taking place. They fail to set the stage for the reader.

What type of film is the hardest to write?
The most difficult writing of all is comedy. Very few comedic ideas work well on paper. Comedy is so dependent on mood and individual experiences. It's tough to make it happen in a script.

What problems with developing plot do you see most often?
There is a tendency among newer writers to forget that they're on a linear progression. Instead, they frequently get off on a sidetrack they find interesting, and by the time they get back to business, it's too late. They want so much to impress you with their writing skills that they forget that writing a script is about telling a story.

Any tips for developing plots?
Be clear.

What about the three-act structure?
Depending on the customer, scripts can be any number of acts. Selling scripts is about the first ten pages. Make them sing. If you don't get the first ten pages right, no one will finish it.

What about dialogue?
It's usually unimaginative. Characters say the same things over and over. Because as a society, we've given up reading, we don't expose ourselves to dialogue and ideas that can be incorporated into our own speech. So most writing lacks originality.

Going to the movies and watching TV doesn't help. You have to read. It doesn't have to be the classics. It can be technical material, military history, anything that might help you understand how people in different walks of life think and talk.

How can writers know when their characters come alive on the page?
Always through dialogue. If they speak in an interesting fashion, that conveys much more than any situation you can put them in or physical attributes you can give them.

What about well-written scripts with no idea and poorly-written scripts with a great idea?
Sometimes a good piece of writing comes without a story to hang on it. I have never bought a script that fits this description. Conversely, I have found, and on occasion bought, scripts with a good idea, but unimpressive writing. An interesting idea can overcome a lot of problems.

Any general advice for writers?
All writers should have backup skills with which to make a living. Learn how to operate a Caterpillar or do people's taxes. You need to eat while you're working toward success. Waiting on tables may sound romantic, but it's a tough way to make ends meet. Get a good job, and then write in your spare time. Your scripts will be better when written on a full stomach.

Writers also need to learn to sell, to pitch. Too often, writers like the process of writing, but when it comes to pounding the pavement, they leave it to an agent or a lawyer, or they blindly send out their material. You've got to be you own advocate, to learn how to command a room when you enter it and control it while you tell your story.

Do you believe the popular wisdom about making it in five or ten years?
I don't believe any of that crap. There are no such rules. Success can come with your first script, your fiftieth, or never. The only sure thing is that if you don't try, you're guaranteed to fail.

STUART OKEN
Stuart Oken has been in the movie business officially since 1985. Currently a Senior Vice President of Creative Development for Disney's

theatrical division, as a producer, Stuart has been involved in the films, *About Last Night*, *Queens Logic*, and *Impromptu*. In his current position, he finds and develops stage projects.

What's the first thing you notice when you pick up a script?
How well it's xeroxed and how long it is.

What's the most important script element for you?
Story and character are equally important.

What is the most common script problem you find?
The biggest shortcoming—and this is not a criticism of individual writing but of the system—is that if the script doesn't scream "MOVIE," it probably won't be made into one. Most ideas are easily dismissed, even if they shouldn't be. The central idea of the film must be unique enough to create promise that it will actually get people out of the house and into a theater.

What turns you off to a script?
If the writer creates characters less intelligent than the audience. It also has to be truthful. If I see human behavior where I can't connect the dots, I lose interest.

What type of film is the hardest to write?
Comedy.

What problems with developing plot do you see most often?
Every story has plot problems. They're usually fixable. The hardest thing is to come up with great ideas and characters.

Should scripts be written in the three-act structure?
Not necessarily. They should have a structure you can hang a story on, but it needn't be any one approach.

Which is the most important act to get right?
Hard to know. If it's a spec, no one's going to read much past the first act if you don't get it right.

How important is character development?
Subject to the idea being worth pursuing, character development is everything. I often start with a character. If you choose to do that you also have an increased chance to derail.

What about dialogue?
If it's funny, it needs to be serious, and if it's serious, it should also simultaneously be funny. Dialogue needs to be crisp, witty, and intelligent. No big problem!

What about premises and themes?
My only criterion is that it has the potential to be entertaining. Then, if a script is well written, I ask myself, Can I sell it, and do I want to spend a year of my life making it?

How do you view your job?
My job is to create high-caliber entertainment that gets people in the seats. If, in the process, we can make a deeper statement about our lives, okay. But ultimately, if an audience walks out of a movie completely unmoved on every level, we've failed.

Any general advice for writers?
Keep writing, thinking, and reading. Be pragmatic enough to understand the marketplace you're writing for. But don't be afraid to fail. Taking risks is generally the way to come up with something special.

To succeed, however, you have to have 1) luck and 2) longevity. Keep your overhead down and write. There are exceptions, but don't live by exceptions. Live by the rule.

And remember that producers are at the bottom of the food chain. We have enormous trouble trying to get people to respond to our projects. There aren't that many buyers, and fewer and fewer of them are artistically driven.

JOAN BOORSTEIN

Joan Boorstein, currently the Senior Vice President of Creative Affairs at Showtime's Entertainment Division, has been in the business about fifteen years. After getting her degree in English and Drama from New York

University, Joan began as a research executive on *The Big Blue Marble*. From there, she moved to Vice President of Acquisitions for Show-time, and then to Vice President of Creative Affairs. In her present capacity Joan's been involved with *Paris Trout*, *The Wrong Man*, and *Keeper of the City*.

What's the first thing you notice when you begin a script?
I notice if the opening scene captures my interest and whether there's an action sequence or interesting character. That encourages me to look further.

What script problem bothers you the most?
Fake characters. If the characters don't sound true or they use stock dialogue or if they're motivated by plot rather than by their interior life, these things are serious shortcomings.

What is the most common script problem you find?
Characters that seem to be generic, formulaic. And too, too often, plot and character aren't intertwined.

What type of film is the hardest to write?
Comedy.

What problems with developing plot do you see most often?
Mostly I see implausible behavior and plot lines that are lost and never found. Sometimes you see endings tacked on for effect, rather than being a part of the story.

What should writers consider when developing their plots?
After they finish, the scriptwriters have to sit down and track the entire script to make sure character works throughout. Don't do it before you write, or you'll edit yourself too much.

What about the three-act structure?
It seems to be a workable approach. From a development perspective, you need to get involved in the story from the beginning, but all acts are equally important.

What about the importance of character?
To me, good characters are essential. That's what the story's about—people. Interesting characters make a story unique.

Writers need to pay more attention to who their characters are, instead of the next plot beat. If they do, their characters will take them in more interesting directions.

Any reaction to dialogue?
Too much dialogue is full of clichés, and too often, the voices of all the characters sound alike. There's no individuality.

Any tips for writing dialogue?
I'm a big believer in reading lots of books and listening to how different people speak. Keep a notebook of phrases and sentences people use. It can act as a trigger to help get a character's voice.

Any suggestions for finding a premise or theme?
It's something that the writer has to feel really comfortable with and is interested in.

How about the character/plot balance?
I don't think you can separate them out. You need good characters and a good story, although it's harder to fully realize character than it is story.

Do you ever develop scripts that aren't well written, but are driven by a great idea?
Yes.

How does the development process work at your company?
I take pitches and read scripts that are submitted. At Showtime, we get probably thirty scripts a week. I read both recommended and passed-on material.

Is the development process changing?
Except that I get fewer pitches than I used to, it's pretty much the same. I think one reason there are fewer pitches being done these days is that they are riskier. There is not a lot to go on for a development person. And there aren't many people who pitch well.

Describe your job.

My job is finding interesting material and then shaping the scripts by working with writers. I'm able to facilitate the production by creating an environment that's comfortable for directors and writers and by contributing notes to various cuts (versions of the edited film), until we get a final one.

Any general advice for writers?

Write about things you really care about. That's where you do your best work. At the beginning, have a couple of spec scripts that are diverse, so you'll have more than one thing to show. And pay attention to detail. Don't be sloppy about your work.

EPILOGUE

I hope you've learned something or gained a new insight in the preceding pages. At least I hope you've found something you can use as you charge the fortress Hollywood. A dozen times throughout the text, I've cautioned you that succeeding as a screenwriter is a daunting task, not one the easily-discouraged, the artistically-effete, or the self-righteous ought to undertake.

I am convinced your pursuit is worth the trouble. We live during a time of, in James Joyce's words, "The ineluctable modality of the visual." Foremost among our senses, it is the visual that feeds us the world. And for over a century, the moving images we've gazed upon in darkened theaters have given Joyce's phrase an unplanned resonance. Movies are the ineluctable modalities that have molded and sculpted our impressions of people, of the world, of ourselves, and of life.

What writer wouldn't want to be one of the sculptors? Who wouldn't want to be a part of this creative, influential process? For those who are excited by the possibility of being a part of the film industry and have chosen this book as an aid in your efforts, let me leave you with this thought from Goethe, "Whatever you can do, or dream you can, begin it. Boldness has genius, power, and magic in it." Good luck.

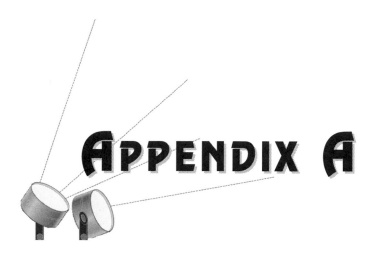

APPENDIX A

BOOKS

So many books on screenwriting have been published in the past few years, it's apparently become a cottage industry of sorts. However, the following list of books, though far from a complete compilation of all the volumes available, are the ones the industry trusts, and any working writer in Los Angeles is familiar with them. Besides, they are the ones I've actually read and found helpful. I've read others; I just didn't think they were all that valuable. Remember, any book is good that encourages you to get to your desk or inspires you to dream of yourself as a writer.

Egri, Lajos, *The Art of Dramatic Writing*. New York:
Simon and Schuster, 1946.
This book's been around awhile, but it's one of those basics that continues to be recommended by everyone. I wonder if all the people who praise it have read it, but then I'm a cynic.

Else, Gerald F. (translator), *Aristotle's Poetics: The Argument*.
Cambridge, Mass.: Harvard University Press, 1957.

Field, Syd. *Screenplay*. New York: Dell, 1982.
Another basic text that is recommended with reservations. While people actually read this volume and claim it helps, everyone also fears that it might encourage formulaic screenplays.

Goldman, William. *Adventures in the Screen Trade*. New York: Warner Books, 1984.
This book ought to be read just for its take on how the industry works and the writer's place in the maelstrom. Goldman's new book, *Which Lie Did I Tell: More Adventures in the Screen Trade,* adds to and updates the material of his previous work. Both are worth the money for their insight into the life of a Hollywood screenwriter.

Lew Hunter. *Screenwriting 434*. New York: Berkley Books, 1993.
This book is material from Hunter's Screenwriting 434 class at U.C.L.A. It's all great, down-to-earth instruction based on his many years of teaching and experience in the business.

Potts, L. J. *Aristotle on the Art of Fiction*. New York and London: Cambridge University Press, 1953.
It's worth your time to read what the original master had to say about dramatic writing.

Seger, Linda. *Making a Good Script Great*. New York: Samuel French, 1988.
This book was by far the most useful book I've read. It is clear, reassuring, and chock full of good advice.

Strunk, William, Jr., and E. B. White. *Elements of Style*, 3rd Edition. New York: MacMillan Publishing Company, Inc., 1979.
Do not pick up a sheet of paper and put it in a typewriter without first knowing this book, unless of course your first language is Tamil or Zulu. If you're looking to make your mark in the English-speaking world, this book is your guide to literacy.

The Bible
This has been the source book for so many story ideas over the years, someone should have the rights to it.

GUIDES

There are a few studio directories published. I've used a couple and found them helpful.

Hollywood Creative Directory, published in Santa Monica, Calif.
This book lists about every production company known to man—at least those in Los Angeles. It lists the studios, the majors, and the networks separately, and it lists the names that go with the production companies. This is a very good starting place for a writer to get an idea of what types of films specific companies make. Editions are released three times a year.

Pacific Coast Studio Directory, published in Pine Mountain, Calif.
The granddaddy of directories, this one has been around longer than most people. It lists agents, production companies, the guilds, where to get animals for your next production, where to find a director of photography. You get the idea. It is probably more useful to small production companies than to writers, but it might also be helpful. New editions are printed three times a year.

The Agency List, published by the Writers Guild.
This is a compilation of nearly all the literary agencies that operate in Los Angeles and around the country. It's worth having one of these lists if you're looking for an agent. Call the Writers Guild to find out how to obtain a copy.

The Writers Guild also publishes a monthly magazine in which they list current television shows, whether they are accepting scripts, and whom to contact at the shows.

MOVIES

Although viewing movies can't help you write or sell your material, there are a few films that you should see if you are serious about getting into the movie biz.

The Bad and the Beautiful, 1952. Written by Charles Schnee.
An oldie-but-goodie Hollywood story about a producer's relationship with a star, a director, and a writer. It's terrific and not too horribly dated, unless you have a thing against black-and-white movies. It won five Academy Awards.

The Big Picture, 1989. Written by Christopher Guest and Michael McKean. Kevin Bacon stars in this story of a brand new writer-director who gets the big rush from status-conscious, but not story-conscious Hollywood producers, and it goes to his head. This is a great view of how Hollywood works, especially as it did at the end of the 1980s.

The Mistress, 1992. Written by Barry Primus.
A producer desperately wants to get a film made. A writer desperately wants to get a script sold and a movie made. The producer tries to set it up with small-time backers. The writer is hopelessly addicted to Hollywood, while the backers care only about making stars of their girl-friends. It may be the most realistic of the lot.

The Player, 1992. Written by Michael Tolkin.
This suspense story about a flaky producer who thinks a disgruntled writer is threatening his life is darkly comic, taking lots of jabs at the process of getting films made the Hollywood way.

ONLINE SITES

Online sites devoted to movie news, reviews, information, and specifically focused on screenwriters are plentiful and changing. Here are a few of the most useful.

Aintitcool.com This site isn't specifically for writers. It's more about news of the business, lots of information on upcoming films—ones that haven't even started production yet—and way too many reviews of films. But hey, it's cool, at least for now.

Hollywoodonline.com This spot focuses on Hollywood news and lots of celeb stuff. Nothing here specifically for writers, although there is a link or two. If you're interested in reading about stars and directors, this is a good place to do it.

IMDB.com The International Movie Data Base can give you lots of information about thousands of films, new, old, and otherwise. It also lists filmographies of directors, actors, writers, and others. What it doesn't do is give you a good synopsis of the story, and what is does give you are too many reviews from whomever wants to submit one.

Movie sites Every time a movie is produced, they now set up their own online site. If you want information on that particular film, here's the place to go.

Screenwriter.com is designed for screenwriters who want to take screenwriting classes, get info on the craft, listen to experienced produced writers talk about their art, and stuff like that. Very useful site for writers.

Screenwriting.com is a great site for screenwriters. It describes itself as a source for writers, with links to a dozen other appropriate sites for writers.

Scriptorama.com Drew's Script-o-rama is primarily a place to download actual screenplays. Doesn't hurt to read some of these to see how the pros work a story. It also has links to other sites.

Besides the above sites, the *Creative Directory*, the daily trades (the *Hollywood Reporter* and *Variety*), the Writers Guild, and other established firms and print journals also have their own Web sites.

APPENDIX B

SCRIPT TITLE PAGES AND OPENING PAGE

THE RED AFTERNOON

An original screenplay

by

George Wryter

Contact:

G. Q. Wryter
0000 W. 100th St.
Dome, AL 00000
(000) 000-0000

THE RED AFTERNOON

by

George Wryter

Based on the novel by Hickory Smith

Contact:
G.Q. Wryter
0000 W. 100th St.
Dome, AL 00000
(000) 000-0000

THE RED AFTERNOON[1]

FADE IN[2]

EXT A LARGE CLASSROOM - NIGHT[3]

Standing in front of a beat-up, old-style chalkboard bordered by the ABCs and children's cheery art work, HARRY,[4] a shabbily-dressed older man, addresses an audience of unshaven bottom feeders and misfits who took every wrong turn life offered. They sleep, smoke, stare.

> HARRY[5]
> I know you don't wanna be here, guys. But we gotta good speaker tonight. (BEAT) So, listen up.

A big YAWN[6] is heard in the audience.

> HARRY (con't)[7]
> Come on now, ya only got an hour.

He wipes his lips with the back of his shaking hand. A nerdy kid, CHRISTOPHER, about 10, carrying a briefcase, walks in confidently. He searches the men's faces.

> CHRISTOPHER
> (adult voice)[8]
> Gentlemen. I represent Kidd Investments. Now's the time . . .

---

[1]The title is centered and capped. Sometimes, it's underlined.

[2]This is capped and used only at the beginning of a script. At the end, use FADE OUT.

[3]Start each new scene by indicating whether or not the scene is interior (INT) or exterior (EXT), the scene's location, and the time of day.

[4]The first time a character's name is given, capitalize it.

[5]When you write dialogue, the character's name is capitalized.

[6]When a sound will be audible to the audience, it is often capitalized. It's not necessary, but it's an old style.

[7]Use the "continued" abbreviation when a character continues speaking after a paragraph of description.

[8]Instructions here are "from the neck up" only. Use sparingly.

APPENDIX C

INTERVIEW DATA

The answers given by the script analysts, development executives, and producers interviewed for this book have been compiled below. The numbers vary, because some people gave more than one answer or didn't answer. The forms of the questionnaire were varied somewhat, depending on where in the development process the individual worked. The purpose was to solicit a variety of opinions, not to get quantifiable responses. Therefore, simple answers (agree, disagree, don't know) of the sort professional pollsters seek were not gathered, hence the data below.

GENERAL

What is the First Thing You Notice about a Script?

If the writing is professional	11
The look of the total package	10
The length	9
The overall neatness, typeface, etc.	6
The title	5
If the reader knows the writer	2
Dialogue	1

What is the Most Important Script Element to You?

The story/plot/structure	9
Characterization	6
If it keeps you interested	5
Premise/idea	3
If it is commercially viable	2
Everything's important	1
Dialogue	1
Does it have passion	1

What Are You Willing to Overlook?

Everything if it's a great idea	6
Spelling/grammar/mechanics	4
Lack of polish	2
Structure	2
Characterization	1
Dialogue	1
Nothing	1

Most Common Script Problems Seen:

Characterization	7
Story problems	4
Being too derivative	3
Spelling/grammar/mechanics	1
There is no most common problem	1

What Immediately Turns You Off to a Script?

Character problems	7
Story/structure problems	5
Predictability/lack of originality	5
Dialogue problems	4
Spelling	2
Mishandling characters' relationships	1

PLOT

What Plot Problems Do You See Most Frequently?

Problems with storytelling	8
Implausibility of plot	7
Predictability, formulaic	5
Starting story too soon	1
Not starting story on page 1	1

Tips for Constructing Plot:

Carefully work out all plot details	11
Make sure characters are interesting and the source of action	7
Don't forget to establish a tone	1
Ask yourself if the material's entertaining	1
Make it fresh	1

STRUCTURE

Should Scripts Be Written in Three Acts?

Yes	12
Doesn't matter	7
No	4

Which Is the Most Important Act?

All of them	10
Act I	10
Act II	3
Act III	2

DIALOGUE

What Dialogue Problems Do You See Most Often?

Flat, clichéd, dull	11
All characters sound the same	6
Unnatural, pat, or hokey dialogue	3
Too much dialogue	3
Filler or dishonest dialogue	2

Suggestions for Dialogue:

Listen to people's speech	6
Create characters carefully, then listen to them	5
Read, see movies and plays	4
Write as little dialogue as possible	4
Writing dialogue can't be learned	3
Read your dialogue aloud	1

CHARACTERS

How Important is Character in Screenwriting?

The most important element	12
A very important element	6
Depends on story	3
Secondary to plot	2
Not primary	1

Tips for Creating Character:

Make sure they ring true and are realistic	6
Make them interesting	6
Make sure action comes from character	4
Get to know them very well, they'll take care of plot for you	4
Use dialogue to reveal character	2
Use action to reveal character	2
Make the hero likable	2

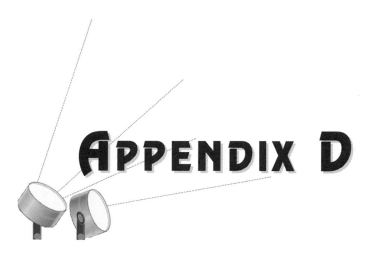

Appendix D

Below is a list of the films from which the quotations at the beginning of each chapter were taken.

Chapter 1.   Dean Wormer (John Vernon), *Animal House*

Chapter 2.   Mark Wallace (Albert Finney), *Two for the Road*

Chapter 3.   Mommy (Jane Atkins), *Mr. Mom*

Chapter 4.   Terry Malloy (Marlon Brando), *On the Waterfront*

Chapter 5.   John Foster Kane (Orson Welles), *Citizen Kane*

Chapter 6.   Claus Von Bulow (Jeremy Irons), *Reversal of Fortune*

Chapter 7.   Joe (Cary Grant), *Mr. Lucky*

Chapter 8.   The Judge (Liam Dunn), *What's Up Doc?*

Chapter 9.   Harry Lime (Orson Welles), *The Third Man*

Chapter 10.   Emperor Joseph II (Jeffrey Jones), *Amadeus*

INDEX

BOOKS FROM ALLWORTH PRESS

Selling Scripts to Hollywood by Katherine Atwell Herbert (softcover, 6 × 9, 176 pages, $12.95)

So You Want to Be a Screenwriter: How to Face the Fear and Take the Risks by Sara Caldwell and Marie-Eve Kielson (softcover, 6 × 9, 240 pages, $14.95)

The Screenwriter's Guide to Agents and Managers by John Scott Lewinski (softcover, 6 × 9, 256 pages, $18.95)

The Screenwriter's Legal Guide, Second Edition by Stephen F. Breimer (softcover, 6 × 9, 320 pages, $19.95)

Writing Television Comedy by Jerry Rannow (softcover, 6 × 9, 224 pages, $14.95)

Making Independent Films: Advice from the Filmmakers by Liz Stubbs and Richard Rodriguez (softcover, 6 × 9, 224 pages, $16.95)

Producing for Hollywood: A Guide for Independent Producers by Paul Mason and Donald Gold (softcover, 6 × 9, 272 pages, $19.95)

The Writer's Legal Guide, Second Edition by Tad Crawford and Tony Lyons (hardcover, 6 × 9, 320 pages, $19.95)

Writing.com: Creative Internet Strategies to Advance Your Writing Career by Moira Anderson Allen (softcover, 6 × 9, 256 pages, $16.95)

Writing for Interactive Media: The Complete Guide by Jon Samsel and Darryl Wimberley (hardcover, 6 × 9, 320 pages, $19.95)

Business and Legal Forms for Authors and Self-Publishers, Revised Edition by Tad Crawford (softcover, 8½ × 11, 192 pages, includes CD-ROM, $22.95)

The Writer's Guide to Corporate Communications by Mary Moreno (softcover, 6 × 9, 192 pages, $18.95)

Please write to request our free catalog. To order by credit card, call 1-800-491-2808 or send a check or money order to Allworth Press, 10 East 23rd Street, Suite 510, New York, NY 10010. Include $5 for shipping and handling for the first book ordered and $1 for each additional book. Ten dollars plus $1 for each additional book if ordering from Canada. New York State residents must add sales tax.

To see our complete catalog on the World Wide Web, or to order online, you can find us at *www.allworth.com*.